This Island

Portsmouth in Poetry

Sponsors and Partners of This Island City

Spinnaker Press is grateful to the sponsors and partners who helped make this book possible.

Major sponsors:

Portsmouth High School
The News
Fry & Kent Estate Agents
The Spinnaker Tower (Continuum Group)

Individual sponsors:

Alastair Bell (Bell Microsystems)
Jane Robinson
Karen Fricker
Jacqui Mair

Partners:

Jon Everitt (Gonfalon)
Groundlings Theatre Company
Tongues&Grooves Poetry Club
Express FM
New Theatre Royal Poetry Club

This Island City

Portsmouth in Poetry

Edited by Dale Gunthorp
with Maggie Sawkins and Denise Bennett

Consultant Editor: George Marsh
Cover painting and linocuts by Jon Everitt

Spinnaker
Press

2010

First published in 2010
by Spinnaker Press Ltd

www.spinnakerpress.co.uk

22 Wimbledon Park Road
Southsea PO5 2PU, England

ISBN: 978-0-9566619-0-6

Printed by MPG Biddles Ltd, Hardwick Industrial Estate, Kings Lynn, Norfolk
PE30 4LS

Foreword

Portsmouth doesn't get a good press – remember Boris Johnson's quips about drugs, obesity and underachievement? Portsmouth, reports Robin Ford in his poem 'Pompey Town', is seen as a northern town which drifted away and attached itself, tenuously, to the prosperous south coast.

These views have some validity: Portsmouth is a city of stark contrasts – and also of great character. It is the home of the Royal Navy, and has played a heroic role in war and peacekeeping. It hosts royal and naval pageantry. Its Historic Dockyard houses the *Mary Rose*, Nelson's *Victory* and the *Warrior*. The city boasts two fine theatres designed by the legendary Frank Matcham and a first-rate ever-expanding university.

Portsmouth was also a city of fashion, entertaining princes, famous libertines (such as Lord Rochester) and thoughtful people from naval families, like Jane Austen. Dickens was born here; John Pounds, credited with starting the Ragged Schools movement, lived here, and the city's connections include Kipling, Conan Doyle, Brunel, Neville Shute, H.G. Wells and more. Thomas Rowlandson's watercolour, *Portsmouth Point*, vividly depicts its vitality and its bawdiness in the 19th century.

The city's present is also exceptional – Portsmouth, Britain's only island city, exhibits qualities of 'islandness' identified by the United Nations: dense population, family loyalty, the sense of community. Portsmuthians have a powerful sense of ownership of their city, and the people who live in Portsmouth *like* living here. I feel privileged to participate in the life here.

As with many other islands, Portsmouth has a strong tradition of participation in the arts, notably drama, music and literature. The city has produced many fine poets. Yet there has never been an anthology of poems about Portsmouth. There has been no definition of Portsmouth's poetic identity.

This book tries to express that identity. Some of the poems in it are classics. Others were collected from the archives of the city and the Royal Navy; some were offered by well-known poets. Many, the work of poets from all ages and walks of life, were sent in by readers of *The News*, listeners to local radio and members of Portsmouth's poetry and literature societies.

This is a book which endeavours to bring the city to life, showing its character and its people, revealing its scars of war and poverty, and also its beauty. *This Island City* is a first, and I hope that it will be the trailblazer for more and more poetry about this fascinating city.

SHEILA HANCOCK
Chancellor of the University of Portsmouth

Contents

Down time

The lonely city

Looking back

Places

Backwaters

My city

Portsmouth

If this island were a book ...

Slow train to Portsmouth

The sky rinsed as a blue-jean collar,
And the train, on this April Monday, idling,
With nothing better to do than follow
The curves and windings of sidling
Rivers, and, sniffing marsh air, at snail's
Pace clank through the flapping
Washing, proud as *Potemkin* —

Swans glide in flotillas on lapping
Waters, and the estuaries hang up their sails,
Indigo, rust and cerulean,
And clouds, like transfers, soak
On surfaces of inlets where beached boats
Vamp the sun on a morning that floats.

Hamble Halt, Bursledon, Bitterne —
We edge through rushes, inhaling the paint
From upturned houseboats, ketches, yawls,
And hear soon the first faint
Siren notes from Pompey harbour — the train crawls
Past old landing craft, their flaking keels
No longer chipped after raking patrols,
But flopped on the mud like veteran seals.

And I am suddenly returned there,
To a crumbling shore and a barracks where
— Was it in the same lifetime? —
We dawdled between ships, without rhyme
Or reason filling in each day,
Awaiting the signal that would sever
The links, and whisk us from the bay
For an unknown time that might be for ever.

Alan Ross (1922-2001) Cricket writer, biographer, publisher, editor of The London
Magazine, *traveller, sportsman and poet*

City

Planners boast, and pool
the kitty
and slodge their thumbs in all
the rackets;
and the men who really
built the city
sludge pints and pies
in donkey jackets.

Pompey Town

Was roister town, tough, violent, merry,
boozed up to its eyes, inns and alleys
crammed with whores and sailors

still much the same in spirit,
no more press gangs on the prowl, thank God,
shame about the lost fields which lapped
the streets with market gardens, cattle, sheep.

Empire and fashion split the town,
Portsmouth/Southsea, conjoined twins
whose eyes look out on different worlds,
Pompey to barracks, workers, dockyard,
Southsea, its beaches, select facades,
naval gentry settled and discreet
behind their curtains, one-time service streets
now the stews for students, the two connected
somewhere round the funfair by the sea.

This tight-terraced town
some streets stout and steady, others cramped
and junked with bits of cars and mattresses out front,
gutters cracked, windows bleary, all packed tight
on Portsea Island, walled by water till City blew its top
and bridged the channel, flooded up to Portsdown Hill.
The common saw has Pompey as a northern town
which broke away, floated south, moored and settled
in the harbour mud.

I love its faces: correct and naval steady,
arrogant in weathered immobility, flip-side
brassy with streaked hair, tattooes, piercings, rings
hard-boiled eyes and belly laughs.
Ships, salt, jauntiness. This generous, outgoing town.

From a Hillside Seat

From a hillside seat on a misty early evening,
Beyond the residential terraces
Banal at my feet, the city spreads in layers
Of paling grey against a primrose sky.

Monuments to industry and commerce
Dominate; to the right rise the cranes
Of a dockyard Dickens knew, and the four-pointed
Tower of a parish church I cannot name.

Only the sea is clear and colourful.
Only its sparkle answers the low sun.
And looking at it now, I feel its breeze,
Taste its cool kiss of crab and salt.

Portsmouth Sounds

Hilsea sounds like a happy girl paddling in a pool
Buckland sounds trampled by hooves, lordly rule

Wymering sounds like simpering pity where none is due
Old Portsmouth sounds totally different from the new

Copnor sounds like burnished metal and honest traders
Farlington sounds like effort with resplendent failures

Drayton sounds like a blacksmith's dream brewers abroad
Portsea sounds compass round from starboard

Fratton sounds like a chip pan spitting
North End sounds naughty when south end's where you're sitting

Milton sounds like a baby's place
Stamshaw sounds like petulant disgrace

Paulsgrove sounds like a little boy's wood
Highbury sounds like Robin Hood

Landport sounds like an attic entrance
Eastney sounds like a genuflect mischance

Cosham sounds like Hollywood slapstick
Southsea sounds as if it ought to be exotic

The dockyard sounds like a short measure,
And Pompey's the beat of a drum, a sound to treasure.

Tales of One City: 1968

She woke in the City in sixty-eight
escaping kind tyranny of country life
to a Winter Road bedsit

Embraced the possibilities
that hit in the face like spray on stormy days
down by the Hot Walls

The city undressed itself, Albert Road
murmuring touch the honey fur coat, it's yours
for just two pounds

You may buy this mandolin
and pluck its strings and stroke its pregnant belly
wildly dance and sing

Above the waves on South Parade
the lightshow's blobs of yellow pink and green sliding
on the Pretty Things

One night in the architecture block
they slept in a vat of plastic balls, innocents
curled up in their clothes

Walked home in the dawn from High Street
through hard stone towers of Somerstown looming
silent and white

Let's march against this far-off war for truly
you can change the world and nothing bad will touch
this phoenix city

New and sparkling like morning sea
backs of houses chained together with fire escapes
to hold them down.

City Island

Of the island ringed by shingle mud and walls,
There are many who were born here who will die
Without ever setting foot across the shore,

Their whole lives, from the kickoff to last call,
Pegged in roundly to the twenty-some square miles
Of the island ringed by shingle mud and walls.

From its look-out spire with its in-built glass floor,
They can eye the lie, with the tourists, gull high,
Without ever setting foot across the shore.

On the streets, when a traditional crowd brawl
Brings the spice-and-battle history back to life
Of the island ringed by shingle mud and walls,

They are there too, those who know it grit and all,
Know its sludge, have scaled its walls: fight a good fight,
Without ever setting foot across the shore.

Some remain, who only meant to stay a while.
If you ask why — sail, with your freedom, sail wide
Of the island ringed by shingle mud and walls,
Without ever setting foot across the shore.

City Blues, 1983

I walked out last night
in the city streets
and orange streetlamp air
walked out from the executive saloon
where carousing city planners
had congregated with the men
who sign the papers
and walked out from the yawns and yawps
of loungers on expense accounts
and let the swing-doors bang like thunder

I walked out to the wind
and falling smog
bellowed by frosty breath
from west wind cheeks
into my cold cupped hands
I looked up to the cement
and glass-front towers
which blotted out the stars
I descended twenty-seven steps
down to the white-tiled underpass
where a pile of piss and litter
blew against the walls
and black prophetic writings
and a gang of leather jackets
black as bats
with ghost-struck hair
ran screeching down a tunnel
howling in their chains

I made resounding footsteps
through the icy draft
and up the Main Street
where more litter swirled
outside the rattling chain-store windows
which reflected other windows
and a jumbo billboard
with trendy spelling

I walked on down the concrete alleyway
where supermarket trollies

toppled over in the alleys
and died overnight
and more litter swirled
and walked on through the Arcadia
past its modern architectural shapes
sculpted out of mouldering concrete
past the neon strip-lit bowling alley
and on past the wire-thin saplings
rooted in the pebbled path
which leads back to the City Arms

and I sneaked into the public bar
and behind a screen of smoke
were the men with arms like JCBs
who built the city
and who with tattoos like branded bulls
and eyes like upturned beer mugs
were stampeding for a brawl
and so what to do
but turn back out

see what we have done
boast the godless city elders.

Braille City

So I place my hand
over the raised scars
of the South Downs;
sixteen-stitches bunch
in knotted hills.
Downwards I tangle
threads of motorways until
my finger pricks on Selsey Bill.
Along the Witterings
I follow west
over the floating anchor
of Hayling Island,
to Portsmouth.

My index finger draws a grin
from its shape — right to left.
My old road leaves a splinter.
As my thoughts linger on the seaside city
my palm rests on the rough diamond,
my fingers drum the water
that separates one from the other.

DALE GUNTHORP

An Accidental Island

When there's salt on your pillow and wind in your eyes,
when the tides rise four metres and the land only three,
and the beach is the graveyard of a billion tiny lives,
your city seems a narrow perch –

where low-hulled ships whisper a nuclear statement,
as they slink past a shoreline of deserted battlements
and then moor by a warship, the relic of a tyrant,
innocently named Mary Rose.

Is there fear over Gunwharf or up on the terraces
of the forces that made you, and will one day unmake you?
As your bed slowly slips in the mud of old glaciers,
does the sea sigh 'matchwood, matchwood'?

What will you do, you people of this Atlantis island?

> 'What hey! We live on the edge, we folk
> of this garrison town. Bombs shattered the dreams
> of our mothers; the prayers of our fathers choked
> in small boats off Dunkirk.

> 'For our children, unskilled and jobless, the reason why
> lies in bottles and needles, fistfights and football –
> till in holy terror, banging their gongs, they cry
> "Jesus, remember me".'

Red Arrows tint the skies of our pockmarked island.
Waves brighter than gull wings soar over the sea wall.
The planet trembles like a hamster in your hand,
yet stumbles on through space –

> 'God of Portsmouth, we cry to thee
> for those in peril from the sea.'

JOHN DE PREY

Port's Mouth

Much that's frightening about the English
began and ended off Spithead.
It is the blooded maw of England. You can see it
now in monumental names and weighty
pages of history, the gold-braided pitiless glory of war
won by unthanked spent lives, maiming and misery
beyond tears – bent old tars chewed, spat out
and forgotten; boys who never came back.

You'd never think it now, with its parking permits,
light-flooded malls, poster ads and petrol stations
the same as anywhere. Maybe it's best seen
hazy with beer, or smelled at the water's edge,
or heard in the silence of absence.
Portsmouth, the mouth that snarled, now
as always, sighs deeply for the passing
of ships and souls, the flotsam of power.

Portsea

If this island were a book, on the margin the sea
would write dedications to a far country;
histories would thunder on the fly.
The present may be written there by day
but the past is new pressed at night.
                    I would still come here…

If this island were a cathedral where the spirit is
a fleeting trick of air and water and edifices
and of a congregation that never enters, never leaves;
where the only sermon is the wind from across
the harbour to which I listen but cannot hear
                    I would still come back…

If this island were a month it would be January.
All gifts given, full of resolutions half-broken before
I made them, when I came in this two-faced month
with its blind eye turned in or turned away,
to stand over the desolate water at the dock
                    I would wait here…

If this island were my only sanctuary
where everything is permanent white, ashen, hoary;
where even the swans in pairs or in pity flew North
and it's no good my waiting for their homecoming,
down the swan's road they have taken their constancy
                    Yet I would still come here…

What made this my mainland makes it an island;
chalk cliffs behind and the out-there ahead.
I see shadows passing, depreciating, yet I can read
the book of us by sea-light and by contour. The road out
is also my way in, even without right, more without reason
                    I will still come here to find you.

People

Dressed up as a queen all day,

I play hopscotch

haiku

this solid glass floor
children look down when they jump
leap into the known

Richard Williams

in the rose garden
a man I don't much like
enjoying the sun

George Marsh

night clubbing:
the promenade's fairy lights highlight
the glass in your hair

Anthony Rollinson

drugged up to the nines
swaying atop the Big Wheel
candyfloss kisses

Mia Ficton

on the beach at dawn —
last night's heart
washed clean away

David Bell

The History of Me

The history of me
is that I was born
in St Mary's Hospital
on a bed
with my mother
and my father.
But I sort of wish I had stayed
in that lovely wet belly
where I swam about.
But I enjoyed looking
for the very first time.

(Peter Jacobs then aged 7)

Our Street

Dressed up as Queen all day,
I toss fivestones, play hopscotch.
Elvis vibrates from the open doors of railways houses.
Aproned, arms folded, women scowl and mutter
'Out with a different sailor each night
and her girl dead of diphtheria'
only a fortnight since.

Girls in Start-rites push bald dolls in prams.
The grocer pours sugar into cones of folded paper,
cuts a shilling piece of Cheddar.
An Austin Seven turns a corner.

I see Calliper Boy stumble, born too early for
the school nurse with Mr Salk's vaccine
on a sugar cube,

the thin girl with bruises
and nine pale brothers and sisters
who live on bread and syrup.
She wears a frilly ringworm cap,
a candle drip of snot
as she endlessly bounces
a rubber ball against our wall,
putting off
going back for tea.

Natural History
(Cumberland House)

Dear Miss — whose name I can't recall,
who took my childhood eye and made me see
primary colours, yellows, reds and all
the blues that make up sky and sea.

All those days you took us out of doors
to dip our feet in velvet spits of sand,
to crunch the shale, find flotsam on the shores,
cuttlefish, dead wood, a seaweed strand

and rock pools at low tide that teemed---
how much I didn't know or understand
but hoped I should and be like you, dreamed
to hold such naïve creatures in my hand.

Cumberland House whose parquet floor
grew dusty from crepe soles straight off the beach.
We stood and stared at specimens in awe,
stuffed and mounted, silent, out of reach.

Foxes, rabbits, mesmerised in glass,
forced into unnatural display
where voles and field-mice frozen in false grass,
were next to owls who thought of them as prey.

In the last room, the ultimate distaste:
giant spiders, beetles, moths in flight
pinned forever yet crawling in their haste
to writhe away or scuttle out of sight.

A cross section of species and the knife,
a pupa, chrysalis and butterfly.
You told me of their brief but gentle life
while I screwed my eyes tight and didn't cry.

Although your name and face elude me now
I still see these, so glad you taught me how.

Noises

Football going bang
on the ground and in the net,
the breeze whooshing,
the big boys chatting,
the flowers growing,
birds singing,
a fire engine nee-naw-ing,
a bus beeping.
I'm sort of happy.

(Ben Hessey, then aged 5 / 6)

If two mowers mow three fields in five hours...

I'd never taught a class before. There was that shock
when all the faces looked up white at once
the hiss and knock and squeak of my own chalk,
across the blackboard Mr Wayne had asked
the monitor to damp wipe with a cloth
before I'd come in with the register
he'd sent me through the post, ten pounds a week,
and Mr Wayne himself beyond his thin
partition, Mr Wayne who, when the noise
rose in my room would slit the door a crack
and there was just his glint of specs, then every
pupil bent and frowning at his book,
or he'd come striding in waving his cane
the faces whitened as he went between
the rows and thwucked and slashed across their backs,
then from the shadowy rear of the room,
his head half tilted back to make the glasses
focus on the board, rapped out a question
then a name, and then the boy would stare
ahead, then shut his eyes, then stare again
*because you were not listening, you **were**
not **were** you, boy?* pause, then timed with the cuts,
pay — ing— a — ten — tion!
and me, when he had gone, *I am ashamed
of you, Class Four — that Mr Wayne had had to. . . .*

Dan from the class above said what you do
is pick the biggest one first day, give him
the cane, and then the rest'll settle down.

The failed eleven plus boys whose Dads hoped
that Mr Wayne's academy might yet
deliver them a Dockyard Exam pass
through me, the dropout with a need to boost
my CV, and to get to Training College —
all those fields and hours of mowing acres
that the rule of three man laboured at
for no good reason but providing problems
that in real life he wouldn't have
yet I still had to calculate at home
by starting from the answer in the back.

Down to Portsmouth

Miss Powell had thick legs.
Neighed like a carthorse.
She did the Infants
so you never noticed how glossy
her mane was when she laughed.

Miss Thomas was little and spry.
Like a bird you'd think but boy!
she had a tongue on her to shave wood.
Lumping great kids at the Elementary
ate from her hand.

Down from Wales to Portsmouth,
came to do their bit.
Bombs flew like turnips
thumped in the back of a cart,
tornpaper wildfires crackled.

Fireweed, they called that rash of purple
on the bombsites. Used to make
Miss Thomas and Miss Powell think
of proper flowers. Used to make
that tough little madam
Miss Thomas cry and Miss Powell
stroke the back of her neck
with a gruff hand. Neat
as a pin, their two rooms.
Good china. Found a chip, later,

with mauve flowers you could
see through. *Shame —*
said the fireman after the bomb.
blast must've blown their nighties
right off...

clasped together, *naked*
as the day they were born.

The Unattended Toothbrush

In Fratton I am to present poems in the school of a teacher called Bjørn. As he and I cross the busy, buzzy morning break-time throng, I look downwards and there it is: long and blue and wrong. 'That's odd'. I nod brushwards, but Bjorn is elsewhere and beyond the truth of the toothbrush.

Later in the morning, bashing out my schoolhall verses, I suddenly want to know, 'so did anyone see the toothbrush in the playground today?' A solitary hand makes its way tiredly upwards. The owner is surprised to look around and understand himself to be the only other witness to the misplaced lavatorial accoutrement. We have unexpectedly bonded.

Who saw the blue toothbrush – only him and John did. I sense my younger self beneath – apart from all the others, and with dirtier teeth.

Written after a visit to Priory School, Fawcett Road, Southsea

Cold Harbour

Gentian (with a *g* as in gate not *j* as in gents) is late. He was waiting last night at Gun Wharf Quays. One day, he says, when he's mastered this lingo, he'll have a restaurant of his own.

He takes his place beside me. I lay out the books, explain the aims: to improve pronunciation; to develop understanding. I've brought the local rag. My eyes settle on a story: Two days after his discharge from St James' Hospital, a man has leapt from the A3(M) Bridge. The third this year, and it's only July. The council have put up a sign advertising the Samaritan's number.

I read one sentence and Gentian reads the next. We practice the sounds of the words: *hospital, fatality, enquiry, disgrace*. When we reach the end I ask if this sort of thing happens in his country. That people with mental illness are released into the community before they're ready. He looks past me to the window, begins to laugh. My words hang like frozen rain. *In my country — this*, he says pointing at the paper, *it's nothing. People — all the days are jumping*. I begin to fold the newspaper into a sort of origami boat.

I know, I say, *let's think of a name for your restaurant*. But he's got it all worked out. He's going to call it *Gent's* — with a *g* as in gate. I try to explain why this is not such a good idea, especially in a city like this, where days may already be numbered.

> Driving through hail —
> on the hard shoulder
> a bunch of still white flowers.

Learning English at Friendship House

Although he came from the mountains
(this much I learnt)

he didn't understand
my words for snow.

I fluttered my fingers
in front of him

but he only saw
the wings of birds.

I led him to the window
wrapped myself in my arms

at the shivering sky
but he only stared.

It was slow and involved
the elimination

of sun, wind and rain
but we got there.

Sometimes I think of him
back at the border

I imagine his mountains
their fingers of shadow

the stutter of gunfire
the quietness of snow.

Langstone

Across the marshes, mists hung
low against a dusk sky
the first time we went there.
Down on the shoreline, great hulks
huddled, houseboats deserted, left to decay.

'We have squatters rights,' they said.
The smell of the salty interior,
the musky scent of wet wood,
tattered curtains slapped, sounding
like waves against the bulk.

There were ten of us, two girls
lost among the boys.
Many times that summer we went down
across the mudflats, where our footprints
told us we were the only ones who came.

What I remember is a sense – a touch of regret.
Many of those faces have drifted away
like a summer tide.
But of those I remember I am one of three
left to mourn –

Paula, tomboy, daredevil, vibrant
whose humour cut us like a jagged plank;
died by accident. Steve, carver of weird wood,
much too clever for his own good,
burnt by addiction.

And Phil, the only one who ever kept clean
turned out like a light not out of his teens.
I mourn them now, going down to the harbour
where across the muddy dank smelling water
new houses stand. Monuments to shifting sands.

ANDREW RUDD

A View of the Ferries

Water like polished coal. Across the table
he is still talking. She gazes into the dark,
the harbour below. A street light keeps sparking
on and off. Under the lamp two teenagers
are entwined, absorbed in the discovery
of each other, their tongues exploring
the possibility that loneliness is at an end.

She looks away, into the swirl of the bar, his face.
Begins to taste the moment of his leaving.

They eat at last. The food is passable,
passes. Little remains to say. Under the table
their knees touch in accidental intimacy.
The song of the ferry, deeper than hearing,
vibrates the floor, the optics, the mirrors,

his heart, calling him. She picks up the bottle,
dribbles the last drop into her glass. Ferries
are still coming in, going out, slow and stately,
among the darting pilot boats, enormous
metal slabs, ponderous, symmetrical,
moving into their allotted places without
effort, shining with squares of light.

The Swan Lady of Hilsea Moat

I can tell you her hair is raven,
her eyes owl-like, mouth of rose-hip red.
That she travels into the dark-wood
keeping to the edge of an ancient moat.

How the presence of swans
first announce themselves
as drifting white clouds
the size of children.

In her arms cakes of wheat-bread,
something swans relish
as we might love chocolates,
or cheese, or crisps.

There is a mist they emerge from
as though sweeping out of Avalon
bringing magic potions
with folded wings.

It is at dusk when this happens
and woman and swans
enter the land of mutual love,
exchange tokens.

When she returns to her home
in front of circling photographs of swans
she wears a white dress,
sleeps in white bed-sheets.

Her underclothes purest white –
powders her face into white clouds.

Dream on the Portsmouth Train

I am making a new house
in the old red brick water station.
I see it often from the train:
round windows in its apex.

Hammering in good big nails
for an attic bedroom I feel
each beautiful punch of metal
voluptuously received in hearty pine.

I like this strong. Then I lie
in the bongless place feeling
the wood smell – the new floor
in the old brick full of old heat.

Your long brown hair which should be
grained a little grey, covers my
face and you move up to me
with each breast a star in the west.

My Grandfather and his Sons
('I only had the dream the once, but then I was cut off')

I had a dream, one desperate summer.
I dreamed I saw my grandfather –
Not old, and marked with the wounds of time,
But strong and in his prime,
Dressed in a beautiful black suit, his eyes were burning blue –
Standing in a street in Portsmouth

This Portsmouth, deep in my dream, was strange and rare
Beyond time or heartbreak, filled with shining air

Blue mist swirled around the man I saw,
Flowed into the dark buildings and hidden rooms,
The brilliant sea rose up and reflected a burning moon

The pub sign of the Air Balloon was set with furious names,
The lighted windows were great yellow frames of flame
I heard the secret songs sung in the air

My grandfather's sons stood around him then,
Each with their burning eyes of blue
No sorrow or regret was there
I knew their joy and terror were entangled beyond all unfolding

They turned to me their handsome faces,
My grandfather and his sons
They ran swift as deer away into the shining air,
Vanished beyond my sight

I awoke at once, to the day of care,
I was cut off from the dream I had
Yet in my hand was a silver shell, torn from that spellbound street,
I can feel it still. I can taste its salt

I know the dream will come again
But this time be no dream

The Salvation Army Lady
(I.M. Una Maidstone 1917-2007)

To you who have been
part of my Christmases
for so long, what can I say
when I read in the paper
that you have lately died?

I still see you draped
in December dusk,
dressed in your neat navy uniform,
your Victorian bonnet,
silently shaking your tin
as shoppers drop their coins
within earshot of the band
brassing out the carols
in crisp cold air;

see you standing
with all the strength
and fragility
of a tiny blue winter pansy –
the radiance of your face.

A Salvation Army carol singer outside Knight and Lee in Southsea

A Sort of Bargaining
(from Phillip Larkin's Annus Mirabilis)

We're strolling on the hottest night of the year
between Clarence Pier and the concrete sails
of the Spinnaker Tower when you announce
you're going to buy yourself a new car.

I think of my day sweltering in traffic,
the tropic blast from the dashboard grille of my Astra,
the sun searing my right shoulder.

'I'd settle for air conditioning and electric windows,' I say.
'Well you can't have everything,' is your stock reply,
'I'd settle for someone who communicates and gives me a cuddle.'

I look ahead as the beads of blue light
string us along, take hold of your hand,
think part-exchange, say nothing.

The Hundred Mile Walk

He wore a boiler suit grey as his hair,
perched his slight frame on
the flat cushion of the slatted wooden chair
in that tiny room where the living was done.

Nan would meet him at the garden gate,
proudly say his dinner was on the table.
Acres of mashed potato, greens and stew awaited,
threatened to overflow the vast Woolworths' plate.

In the evening he'd pass a hand over his mouth,
unspoken signal for her to take out
her almost empty purse, toss him coppers
for a pint at The Gordon Arms.

On Sundays he'd say 'Time for our hundred mile walk!'
I'd be silent with awe at the floral clock,
we'd stroll The Ladies' Mile to Clarence Pier,
watch the louche lads on the Waltzer at Billy Mannings.

After my ride on the children's train
we'd pass the War Memorial,
inspect the inclines of the Rock Gardens,
imagine its dull shrubs luridly lit at dusk.

I'd watch fishermen on South Parade Pier,
day trippers lose pennies in fruit machines,
look up at lights above the Promenade,
saving their glory for red open-topped buses at night.

He drink tepid beer in a cool, dark saloon.
I'd sit in a pub garden with my weekly treat of crisps
(salt in a tiny blue twist), glug warm lemonade
at the end of the thrillingest walk of my childhood.

Winter Road

I clutch the warm package,
Wrapped in newspaper,
Close to my chest.
My head is leant forward,
Protection from the rain
Bouncing off the streets:
An act of deference, of prayer.
Water gurgles in the gutter,
It drains from the road
Like a smoker's loosening cough.

I huddle in a doorway and open the parcel.
Chips.
A pile of golden, rough cut chips
Steam in my palm.
Salt and vinegar tease my nose
Driving out the lamp-lit air and wet city fumes.

A hot chip brings my shoulders
Leaping to my ears,
My tongue to the floor of my mouth.
My breath gasps to cool it.

Someone passes.
They have no umbrella, no coat.
My chip fat smile bulges with greeting.

'Wan' a chip?'
She grins.
'D'you mind?'

God, I love chips:
Easy to offer, easy to accept.
She finishes one and takes another.
I watch her mouth open.
I watch her teeth bite, her lips shine.

Everywhere the Sea

when the sea… is a line of light

Awareness of White

Then one morning you come down to this,
a morning of small bird song,
when the sea is calm,
its bed rippled from a gentle sleep
when even seagulls day-trip somewhere else...
while the tide is turning
the way it does
with the small breaths of one still asleep
or half asleep; and the daylight, too,
only half awake and muted.

You come down to an awareness of salt
while by the shore the water is waiting.

Then later as different as sudden as temper,
challenged by the wind, stirred up by clouds racing...
and maybe it is evening or later in the year
and you come down to this...
the beach gorse flattened to green streaks
on burnt ochre and umberish stones,
gravel piled in drifts, as terraces and ditches
while the tide turns out with deep breaths,
with a haunting and real bluster.

An awareness of white,
in unlimited shades.

Portsmouth Harbour
(at 8.45 p.m., 7ᵗʰ July 1971)
          A note to Vera

It is cool now, with a slight breeze
rippling the water.
I bring beer from the Lone Yachtsman
and I sit on a bench with your absence
as my companion.
I know you will be happy here
and that thought calms me.
So I am content to look
and take my fix on the future.
The sun goes down on the Solent,
a golden submarine submerging
to leave its wake trembling
in a path to another world
that could tempt a tourist dreamer
to walk his miracle across.
Faintly, beautiful in the distance,
a sad bugle sounds
to the lowering of flags:
an old sailor remembers
and spits the lump in his throat
into the dark gathering water.
The sun completes its stately descent
and the blushing complimented sky
fades slowly to twilight to beckon stars.
I finish my beer watching a small cruiser
sail on a light breeze towards a calm sea.

The Night Fishermen

Along the littoral
a tentville of umbrellas
on black alert.

Moving torches
at forehead height. Fishing-lines
on dark graph paper.

Incoming waves
leave a snaggle of tooth-marks,
the lick of France.

A late dog-walker
keeps off the beach.
Behind enemy lines.

Sea Wall after School

The row of cars in Clarence car park rocks in a gale.
Facing bright blue sky, cradled inside, elderly folk
with hats on, suckle tea from thermoses and watch.

Eyes narrowed, coat ruffling, leaning to the wind,
braced fours, grip-clawed; up the path a dog
guards his home-dry distance, also on the watch.

Two children (the watched) with Clarks and socks
dumped, hop foot to foot, pink-soled on the spot
where the path, and the wall, are fresh wet.

Warm in their uniforms (name-labels stitched),
they wait (passing boats tilted on foam and chop)
for this up-whooshing spume-tower splattering

laugh-more-than-squeal squeal-more-than-laugh
down to them scattering smile to the pensioners
jump to the dog, shiver and puddle splash-landing.

KATIE NELSON

On Eastney Beach

Pigeons on the stones,
seagulls on the sea,
look at everything
swimming round me.

(Katie Nelson, then aged 7)

Ferries at Southsea

At George's, we see the ferries coming in,
huge trays of light buoyant in the dark blue evening,
floating out of the night towards the palm trees,
towards the young drunk spraycanning the pavement,
his words sputtering away. We watch the ferries,
coming in, their unsteady flickerings like poems,
freighted with the dead, the living and the refugees,
carrying those who don't mind the long way over,
lotus-eaters or dreamers or souls returning,
lit up and floating, like lights themselves,
like the strings of lights that curve and stretch
along Clarence Parade, lighting us to our cars
when we leave at midnight. Soon those night-travellers
will disembark too, dragging their rucksacks
down slipways, smuggling their talents through customs,
dreaming firm ground under their feet,
dreaming, as they try to enter a new berth,
of their children in safe houses
in quiet streets where nights can be dull,
and the only flash is the flash of a car's light
on the elder flowers, crowded and sultry.

ARMANDO HALPERN

Sunset at Southsea

At the island before the island
that taints the edge of the horizon
of a solid cloud hovering over the sea,
across the houses, across the green beach
on the grass where seagulls settle for the night,
at the flint shore, so protected
that the sea is not felt as sea,
there is a line of light.

There, the air is pure
and stains the eyes with the slow colours
that never should be seen.
We open the oyster of the heart
to the nameless emotions that made us,
as simple as water, salt and stones,
outward like a city encircling the harbour,
and we are dreamt into silence
by the free flight of the other birds.

Spithead

Breakwaters
enclose the shore.

Out to sea
celadon-glazed forts
guard Portsmouth harbour

and the sky
is dinosaur boned

.

Equinox

It's raining again in Portsmouth,
but in September we shrug our shoulders,
pack away the tent, and light
the first fire of autumn.

Threads of sky weave a smoky blanket
across the park, and the ground stirs
with the salt of driving tides,
a dash of seaweed, no fish.

Wolfish waves, awakened
by the whiplash of hurricane tails,
hunt across the Gulf.

Sailing off the Camber

The colour of sound –

Wind heavy with pale sand
chopping at the harbour
scouring inns, houses and me.

Burgees in sinus rhythm,
purple and red neckerchiefs
on silver masts.

The snorting caution of shipping
coming in, the shadowed presence
of naval apparatus.

Gulls – peep-o-day boys –
shrieking, always marauding,
black knavery.

A squall slapping on pilings,
on breakwaters,
a salt lick rasping, eroding,

and then somehow summer
with its public buzz,
its sizzling skin,

a jet stream droning its white tick
across sky just a bit blue.
Over this harbour Jesus never walked

yet fish land miraculous.

On South Parade Pier

Alone on the pier, with every sign
telling me not to jump

there is a strange hypnotic pull
towards the edge,

the swell rising and falling,
adrenalin flow to let go, let go.

Behind me is an unknown town
ahead of me, along that path

of tidal light, lies a greater mystery.
The sounds are the same,

whatever the beach, whichever land
lies to the east, or the west,

the swell rising and falling, water lapping
at the edge, then rising and falling.

Eyes closed, I'm back on every warm beach
I've ever known, pinned by the call of the sea.

Anniversary Pages

A cormorant missiles across the Solent.
Flash of white then streak of black,
like sidewinders over San Carlos,
the tipping point between air and sea.

Charcoal smudged on the horizon line.
A greyed-in queue of waiting tankers,
once anchored in the channel swell,
will foghorn chorus the night away.

So sleep now sleep the gently rocked buoy,
so close to shore so out of reach.
Those flailing waves that circle round,
your drifting dreams in the undertow.

The pencil wake of a fishing boat,
A quicksilver trail that soon dissolves,
is lost for ever as mercury falls.
The undercurrents we forgot to feel.

Just past dawn and pavements glisten,
a salt-stain sea-mist swallows the past.
Island fades first then ghosts of ships,
then finally the whitening bones of a pier.

The hiss of waves on pebbles caressed,
scuffed stones no more the dulling of shades,
shine topaz or amber or sapphire or pearl;
this coarse reflection a cursed veneer.

A solitary car pale headlights dipped
is neatly parked on the esplanade
supplement open on the passenger seat
doors airlocked in readiness

As lone engine runs its dismal cadence,
monoxide love's lost memories swim
in wisps of steam from listless fog
of exiled breath on warming glass.

Horses charge a shuddering surf,
no teenage truculence or growing pains,
but spirit drunk and spitting in rage.
Clouds scurry past as words weep to ink.

Fitzroy Plymouth Portland Wight,
north, north east, force two into nine.
Blue lights and tape a closed off road,
bunting flayed under darkening thought.

Sky furrows down under a snare drum roll,
the song of rain on metal on stone.
A single photo in the *Evening News*,
no hail-shot fury at lightning missed.

Wipers track across a wearying sweep,
a heart-pulse beat as ice bullets flicked
bounce once then twice then stop for good,
wet tarmac encrusted by melting stars.

Coventry Sheffield Antelope Ardent,
South Atlantic storms incessantly churn.
No Man's Fort last navigation call,
your one fixed point between sea and air.

On Southsea Esplanade

Day after day
primes the sea
aquamarine.

A parade of beach huts
glares at the water
now at high slack.

At night
a line of moonlight
glosses the dark.

Groynes at Eastney

At low tide, pushing up through the sand,
pale groynes, rubbed round like my grandmother's hands,
whorled stories, twisted fate, beautifully worn
with the endless ebb and smash of small realities.
No bland smoothness here, my fingers feel each line of grain,
and on the ragged tops, the rings which mark the years,
grooved with algae and the tiniest strands of seaweed.
Dark damp seeps up the bleached wood from the sand.
Fingers wait patiently, outstretched to the sky.

Ways of Looking at the Sea

1

The horizon is as straight as a knitting needle.
The knit starts out tight, and gets looser and looser
Until it frays.

2

Someone drew the sea out straight at the top,
And designed it like a skirt. At the
Bottom, the ruffles rustle.

3

The nicest type of tiredness I know
Is after I've been in the sea. The sea
Is my friend. After it has tired me out,
I sleep to the sound of its whispers.

Down Time

The sign hangs high and hinders none,

refreshment take and then jog on

Sitting on Top of a Lamppost

I could feel
the breeze on my cheeks.
When it was late at night
I could see all the rooftops.

I could see
the other lampposts light their way
and I could hear
all the traffic on the motorways.

Up there it felt
like I had my own space.
This feeling in my chest
as if I had space in-
side of me, like everything
had been made around Me —
just for me.

No one else up there. Was there?

(Paul Harris, then aged 8)

At the Kite Festival

He looks shy, with a pale 'tache,
and taking the strain on his thin arms
are wrist-rings like deck-quoits;
he spirals the wing with a stretch
like miming an archer, throws

a thrilling coloured frilled self
into the wheeling flock of kites
and it screams in the air, dances
in the battering it takes; it calms
high up, where the breeze flows

flush across the ribbed and finned,
and streams tails like the King's lances
at the Field of the Cloth of Gold,
signs of his pride and wealth;
but dive it, at right angles, it'll roar

like a thrashing mainsail
as in Chuang Tzu's metaphor
for some power that will wail
through the shy and proud of the world,
our best words ribbons in the wind.

The Wild Mouse

There they are!
My mother and father
chugging along
the steeply rising track
        in their little red car.

She's sitting behind him,
her legs drawn up –
the wind's whipped
        candyfloss into her hair.

I can see the back
of my father's white shirt,
his tattooed hands
        gripping the bar.

Soon they'll reach the bit
where the nose of the car
        juts out over the sea –

my mother will close
        her eyes and scream.

Then the car will jack knife
on its rickety rail,
dive down
and down
as if to crash
        right into the crowd.
        As they whizz past
I'll look up and wave
(my heart's on my sleeve!)
        but they'll be holding on so tight
           they will not see.

Drawing Shadows at the Rec
(for Mel, Claire, David, Beau, Simon and Paul)

The brick street is straight and flat and square.
The boys saunter down the street totally at home
and turn the corner for the Rec. It's a sly change
all green leaves and butty grass in iron spears,
daisies peeping white and yellow bellies.
The sun is melting the leaves a bit, they are soft.
Mel is drawing in grass with bangled hand rushing
to catch the shadows before they change.
Claire is working hard in the playground at her shade
and the four adolescents are getting on
with each other! I see Simon holding a branch
for Beau to draw. Paul, silent as the grave,
is drawing his shoe where each eye is fixed on
the paper by a circle. David is drawing
the light in his water bottle. The light is fierce
on the white page and it wobbles and tipples
all the time so he can't catch it. We try to burn
the paper with the blinding light but 'it don't work'.

Then we go to the graveyard where a past pupil
is buried and under the shadows of the great
poplars and beeches each tells of their blood or
friends buried in that place. Simon becomes deeply
respectful to the point of fear, Beau gets angry
about his young uncle's abandoned monument,
David tells me off for walking across the graves
and Paul is as quiet as the people who surround us,
I can feel their presence in the tears I do not
allow. Claire wibbles a bit at the grave of her friend
buried beneath a dove with Peace in white letters.

David tells us how he saw a white thing one night
but would not go closer. And we walk away, walk
on to what we will do when we die. David wants
no suits, Beau wants lots of colours, Simon will
be burned, Claire has not made a will, Mel listens
sternly and Paul is silent, smiling thinly
in the May sunshine, silent as light in water.

Founder's Day

Take, for example, one muggy morning
I carted off my dreamy soul to Geography
and Mathematics, and had to attend the Cathedral afterwards
in honour of the college founder,
some figure-head the teachers called Saint John.
I sat wishing to myself that this Saint John
hadn't founded anything. I gazed around,
watched some of the speakers,
and made a prayer to Jesus of my own.
Then in that tormenting, wasteful, dreary hour
all my meditations turned
from *Per Adua ad Gloriam*
(if I hadn't got the Latin wrong)
to the glory of my wet and dry trout flies:
the Pheasant Tail Nymph, Red Spinner,
and the Greenwells Glory,
and I thought about the sacrifices
of the evening rise.
      A train-ride home,
and I slouched in through the kitchen door,
let my loaded bag slump off my shoulder:
on the draining-board two fat trout,
the family camera still out of its leather pouch,
my brother's rod and fishing bag
propped against the corner coat-stand,
and his net drying
with a piece of river-weed
strung around its meshing.
Seven and a half uphill-seeming miles
I cycled out to Trotton,
my gum-boots squelching
      underneath the blue sky –
but the crease of line across the water
floated into another evening
for the dark algebra of God's river.

Old Portsmouth Bass

I listened to the humming ferries and squawking seagulls
I hadn't caught a fish all day.
I had half a mind to pack away
when my rod went wiggle wiggle wiggle.
I ran with joy and grabbed my rod.
I tried to reel it in,
but there was a huge force pulling me.
I shouted for help and my dad came and grabbed the rod.
A huge fish jumped out of the shimmering sea!
It was an Old Portsmouth bass wriggling for its life.
It felt like a big slimy worm
and smelt like a ton of fresh seaweed,
its shiny blue eyes were saying Let me go.
We whacked its head against the railings
and dropped it into a bucket of water.
We thought it was dead but it came back to life
and jumped onto the concrete slabs.
We caught it, whacked it again
and put it back into the bucket.
There were no bubbles of breath.
This time it was dead and it wasn't coming back.
I cast the line and stared at the shadow
of the flats on the water and the boats sailing past.
Twenty minutes later wiggle wiggle wiggle.
This time I could reel it in.
A smaller bass jumped out of the sea!
I pulled two hooks from its mouth
and whacked its head three times against the railing.
This fish wasn't coming back.

(Elliot Lyons, then aged 12)

The Dancing Girls of Landport

borne out of red brick corners,
stone, metal, tar and wood

each black shoe has metal on it
clicking wood, clicking wood

inside every tarry shoe
a fine toed foot lonely

to find another foot
that does the same, does the same

with a flack rhythm raining
down on ears like the blitz again

the feet find others cracking
Landport's willow boards

the dancing girls of Landport
elbow-out like wavey sailors

writhe like flames of muscle sprung
by fiddle, box, guitar and drum

a navy gone crazy chuck trouble
aside, hornpipes on land in leotard

crash and smash the wooden floor
to the cobble stones of Landport

South Sea Bubble

(I.M. Hector Ross and June Sylvaine's repertory company,
Theatre Royal, Portsmouth, 1957)

It's fifty-three years, but still present tense though,
ten o'clock, and call, and set the chair
and folding table down front left, watch off
and placed on it, lean back against NO SMOKING,
snap click the elastic bands off script
and pencil as they come in in their slip-ons
and their sweaters from their B and Bs,
and Mel from London to direct, that suit,
that burgundy bowtie. So, write the moves in –
crosses left, switches on lamp sits, - call
them if anyone forgets. And then at lunch
go round among the high stools in the bar
with each one's dressing room this week,
back through the ghostliness of rows of seats
then out into the street to trawl the stores.
If possibly the company could borrow -
last week South Sea squabs, cane chairs, and yes
we'll tape the legs, a programme ad, and please
accept with compliments and bring the wife.
Lighting rehearsal seven-thirty, ladders,
flymen calling to each other high up
out of sight. Quarter to eight, look through
a slit between the tabs: what sort of house?
Then in the mic: Ten minutes, please, Miss Scott,
ten Miss Sylvaine, ten minutes Mr Ross.
And press the button and the houselights dim,
another, and the tabs whir slowly up.
Prompt corner, follow in the script, and watch
in case they don't take in a breath on cue.
And music, phone-ring, light on, doorbell, blackout
all in black on black stage in black gym shoes,
whooshing across like ghosts, each as rehearsed:
hook teapot with a finger, forearm in
through chair-frame, pull the curtains, put on lamps,
alter the clock-hands, and then NOW! And drop
an arm so that the ASM begins,
close to the mic, to tip and roll the peas

across her drum, the hissing back and forth
and forth and back of south sea island surf
beyond the window as the lights fade up.
And near the end of Act Three, this walk-on,
Ali, the servant in brown-face and wide
red cummerbund, the accent, and a grin
of lots of teeth held pausing for the laugh.
The curtain comes down and the clapping dulls,
goes up and it comes back, like interference.
Down again, then up, then just once more,
in front, the seat backs banging, scarves and coats
and lifting elbows, shuffling up the soft
slope of the carpet, towards green lit EXIT
while the safety curtain, that fourth wall
again whirrs down NO SMOKING, click-clunks, locks.
Strike set and sweep stage, check props, eat up
the bread slices and orange domes of tinned
half apricots that had been breakfast eggs,
empty the glasses of cold whisky tea.
Last, check the dressing rooms (once somebody
had killed himself). Then lights. Then lock stage door.
Wait by the theatre steps and columns till
the bus's headlights frame me on the foyer
window in my duffle coat and jeans.

And now the driver's silhouette against
the Guildhall steps, Commercial Road, North-End,
Hilsea, the peaked conductor with his steel
machine to zip my single ticket out,
now Portsdown Hill, The George, Widely, Purbrook
and just me left among the dim-lit seats.

(Title taken from a play by Noel Coward, first performed in 1951)

All's right on the night

> The spotlight shifts
> the silence waits
> for me

But first, the strange daytime of the theatre. This shadowy, womb-like place. This untidy, slumbering contrivance.

Gilded nymphs and putti, mermaids and seahorses, swagger across the front of the dress circle of the Theatre Royal. Comic and tragic masks emblazon the civic box. The orchestra pit is fanfared with drums and trumpets. Above 'the gods' from whence the spotlights play a dusty Father Time.

Flimsy scenery waits to be solidified by skilful lighting. Scrawled on the stage itself are the chalk marks from which the different actors will tonight declaim their lines. Scenes and parts of scenes are being rehearsed with an off-handed indifference. The director is slumped in the pit, slouch hat and hooded eyes. Alert, lethargic, others sit around and come and go. Stage-hands, lighting engineers and who-knows-what wander on and off the stage with easy familiarity. Disarmingly, they treat me as one of them.

Backstage is a labyrinth of stairs and passageways. And here are the curtained wings, from which I shall shortly enter and exit. Stepping in a moment from a shadowed reality into a brightly-lit illusion. Beyond the footlights a sea of faces, a hush of expectation. The stage manager senses my anxiety:

> Stand on your mark
> and say your lines
> that's all

DENISE BENNETT

Wyllie's Boat:
Portsmouth Museum

Looking at his dinghy,
the blue peeling paintwork,
curve of the hull, I taste
the salt air, feel the squall,
see the artist Wyllie
sailing his craft off Spit Fort
taking from the deep
his ardour for seascapes.

Unlike Turner, his hero,
his pictures hold no symbolism
only the pure passion
of waves washing his canvas;
a man rowing in the Solent
catching a crab, racing –
the energy of wood and water
natural to him.

Marvellous how he built
and launched this small open boat,
lifting his oars
propelling it windward.

(William Lionel.Wyllie (1851-1931) was a prolific and successful marine painter. His
13-metre panorama of the Battle of Trafalgar hangs in the Royal Naval Museum at the
Portsmouth Historic Dockyard)

The Lady of the Lake
('Effigy of a Barbarian Queen' by John Hutton, Portsmouth City Museum)

Her arms are folded:
is it in defiance,
or defence, or power?

Guinevere-like,
a mystic Queen in robes of splendour,
etched on glass.

The sword of Arthur
was given to the water and the custody
of the Lady of the Lake.

The lake of glass
where she waits, arms folded
beneath the mirrored sky.

I gaze through her
to the door; she sees through me
as I scribble my notes.

Her eyes follow me
as I leave; on impulse at the door
I turn.

And she has turned.
I see through her to the window;
she sees through me

to the corridor
where stands the ever vigilant
armoured knight.

Portsmouth's Looking Glass

Methinks I see you, newly risen
From your embroider'd bed and pissin;
With studied mien and much grimace,
Present yourself before your glass,
To varnish and smooth o'er those graces,
you rubb'd off in your Night Embraces.

(John Wilmot, Earl of Rochester (1647-1680), a friend of King Charles II, was a reknowned libertine, known for his vivacious converstation, impromptu verses 'extravagant frolics' as part of the 'Merry Gang')

The Animals

Pink sweatered and pigtailed,
Sweetly simpered Sophie:
'Time to slip in a port
Before social and political thought?'

He was sixteen that night in far Eastney
When he'd last had that unstudied charm.
He'd been to her room. It was awful.
She said she loved John Coltrane,
And she'd like to hear more about this Ray Charles ...

Two weeks since that historic tutorial
When he'd called her something unsubtle
In his, he only just then realized,
Throaty deep south salty vowels.
She'd welcomed the icebreaker, actually.

His short for a student hair
And upfront proletarian erudition
Fascinated her.
He thought, she's worth shagging,
Though I'd hate to meet her mother.

So he swallowed his pride
And drank with her:
Dubonnet and Boddington's,
The odd couple ...

Her animal rights badge flashed in fashion-accessorial seduction,
While his animal passion raged toward satiation,
And the wild Animals scorched through the maudlin afternoon:
SOMEDAY BABY I AIN'T GONNA WORRY MY LIFE NO MORE.

Albert Road

Friday night on Albert Road. The dog walkers,
mums and long-marrieds are gone, the decibels
up. Under orange moons, the unchaste hunt
in packs, bare shoulders, black straps and heels
belie these late night prowls.
From the kebabs and fried chicken of Fawcett Road
to the clubs of Waverley, the shrill cry of want
merges with the footsteps and laughter of the herd.
Along the streets, sea breezes ease the air,
bouncers sniff and cough, and taxis glide silently past.

Things to do around Southsea

Sit on the bench where Steve Tebb, Drainman of Portsmouth, sat.
Watch the dancing sea.
Reminisce the Wild Mouse, the Wall of Death,
Uncle Charlie's tattoos.
Get married for the third time.
Launch a book of poems.
Drink champagne at The Queen's.
      Go for a curry.

Watch Syd Little in Cinderella at The King's.
The Spinnaker Tower lit up for Christmas.
Love Albert Road!
Shops full of bling.
      Go for a curry.

Take Amber Leaf and six Milky Ways to a friend in St James's.
Think about the woman they found at the back of Waitrose.
Lend someone a score.
Talk to seagulls.
Play crazy golf.
Listen to the cursing sea.
      Go for a curry.

Take a red geranium to Bett at St Vincent's,
watch Des O'Connor on plasma TV.
Fly a kite on the common.
Consider a swim.
      Go for a curry.

Watch Red Arrows draw love hearts over South Parade Pier.
Buy okra and cardamoms from Akram's for later.
Put change into the Bangladeshi welfare tin.
Collect Robin from the hover.
Inhale the sea.
Have a glass or three at The Florence.
Talk about times.
Love Albert Road!
      Go for a curry.

See Angelhart Quartet at The King Street Tavern.
Disgrace yourself in an Aqua taxi.
Sleep it off.
Write a poem.
      Go for a curry.

The Traveller's Rest

We drank in the Stag and the Lamb & Flag
  in the Harrow and the Royal Oak too,
In the Yorkshire Grey just across the way
  and the old Red White & Blue
In the Surrey Hotel, pretty girls as well,
  they were First and Best in the Air Balloon
Up the old Crow's Nest,
  in the new Full Moon,
In the Fifth Hants Volunteer Arms
  and the Brewers and the Still & West
    And the Traveller's Rest

  (Chorus)
  The sign hangs high and hinders none,
  refreshment take and then jog on
   From the old Traveller's Rest

We played in the Harp and the Marsh and the Rose,
  at the Racehorse won our bet
In the Barley Mow it was time to go
  or we'd be playing yet
It's a Mystery, all the beer was free
  in the Newcome Arms and the Shepherd's Crook
Oh the Pompey Chimes,
  Old House At Home
In the Fifth Hants Volunteer Arms
  and the Brewers and the Still & West
    And the Traveller's Rest

  (Chorus)

From the Mile End Cellars to the Coal Exchange,
  Oyster House to Star
From the old Black Dog to the Smoke Room fog,
  in the Wheelbarrow to Mars
In the Jolly Taxpayer, we sat alone,
  we wept and sighed for the pubs that died
For the Dog & Duck and the good Lord Clive
  For the Blacksmiths Arms and the Hearts of Oak *[ad lib]*
For the Fifth Hants Volunteer Arms
  and the Brewers and the Still & West
    And the Traveller's Rest

  (Chorus)

The Local

So I find myself here again, and I wonder why this time,
because it closes early?
Because the drinks are cheap? (Yeah right!)
Or because the bar is always empty,
and you can always find a seat? (More likely)
So we have sofas like the ones in our front room,
and the clock is never in plain view.
The bar staff know us by name, and only us…
The hot chocolate is drinkable
and we're of local fame (or so we think)

Maybe we're here so often, for the boats that sail on by,
and the water that ripples with our conversation?
For the opportunities to cry 'Fast Cat' when it arrives. (Childish? Us?)
Or as the tall ships sail past.
I try to conceal the tears that well up in my eyes – sentimental fool.

No. None of these are the reasons that we're in here every day.
And though I could tell you,
I wouldn't want you to take up residence. Not on my sofa.
And though the bar is always empty,
It's a permanence. (We like it that way!)

The Phoenix

It's my first time.
Between tightly packed bodies,
I edge to the bar.
'A pint of Grim Reaper please, Love.'
The barmaid detects the tension
underneath the bravura.
A wry smile flickers across the face
of the regular at my elbow.

One good swig and the music takes over.
Billy Budd is tearing it up at the microphone,
and we're all under the boardwalk with him.
Women dance, spinning on their heels.
On the split screen above the bar,
the pool player doubles the eight ball
in a corner pocket.

In the garden, smokers hunch
against the autumn chill.
while Bolly, the golden retriever,
sleeps in the back bar
waiting for last orders,
dreaming of rabbits on the hill.

Disappearing Pubs

I came to Pompey in '59,
to work without compunction.
There seemed to be a pub or shop,
at every corner junction.

An off-licence or grocer's shop,
or one for fish and chips.
Probably much custom came
from sailor boys off ships.

But things have changed enormously,
the supermarket's here,
to sell you all the groceries,
with newspapers and beer.

The Navy too, has been run down,
the dockyard mateys gone,
and many little corner pubs
no longer linger on.

They've been converted into flats,
where people dwell and dine.
For folk who get a home-sweet-home
these changes seem quite fine.

The Florence here is still a pub
with poetry and song,
but we must heed the warning signs,
I wonder 'For how long?'

Weapons Grade Beer

Way down in Portsmouth there is something to fear:
At the Hole in the Wall they sell Weapons Grade Beer.
Just a couple of sips and you'll have the taste,
But a couple of pints you'll be right off your face.
There is a Grandma who makes it says '5% dead'.
She delivers her warning like a slap round the head.

It tastes a little bit bitter and it's like ginger ale.
When you're drinking this stuff you could wrestle a whale.
But then all of a sudden, when it slops round your belly,
Your eyes go all woozy and your legs move like jelly.
Then dizzy meets fizzy and your burp hits your friend
As you all laugh like hyenas and drive folk round the bend.

By the time the bells ring you'll be singing along,
As you're bouncing off lampposts 'cos your legs are all wrong.
In a couple more hours you'll need more than a bed,
With your Anadin Extra and your big swollen head.
Just a day to remember, and the bit that you'll hate
Is the small tiny writing says 'a week to hydrate'.

In a Portsmouth Victorian terraced street
under the looming stand of the neighbourhood
football stadium, in a bare bay-windowed room
there is silence, attentive, good

that we share with all sentient beings
and rising through it, faintly hopeful at first,
growing full, joy bursts with the one voice
of tens of thousands seeing a goal.

Dear Jess,

The sun shone bright; the air was still;
> out pranced the men in blue;
ticker-tape floated in the brilliant light
> and sharply the whistle blew
> (but not, dear Jess, for you).

And from the off the ball seemed charmed
> the Charlton team felt spurned;
while Pompey players passed it pat,
they stroke it like a favourite cat
> and always it returned.
Poor Charlton, chasing shadows,
> grew desperate and wild
the passes flowed, each tackle rode
('Chamberlain! Well I'll be blowed!'),
thousands of spectators glowed
> turned to their friends and smiled:
this was a day to savour
> to remember down the years
the day when Pompey strolled it
> utterly controlled it
like pitting a racing bike against
> a postie's — without gears.

Eat your hearts out, Revie's Leeds
> and Ajax '72 —
this is possession football
total, fluid football
> and the heroes are wearing blue
> (but I'm afraid it passed by you!)
Every one a genius
> from Butters at the back
through the midfield wizards to wily Walsh
> and darting Guy in attack.

And then it came, as we knew it would
> the first of five at least
> > Ray Daniel spurted down the left
> > > with the friendly ball on a lead
> > he bounced it playfully off a couple of chaps
> > wandering around Fratton in need of maps,
> > > crossed, and Guy drew a bead.

In the net! The Cockneys will be fleeced!
They've hardly touched the ball as yet
a Whittingham hat-trick? Wanna bet?
it's not fair beating them like this —
they ought to be policed.

And so it went in the warm Spring sun,
the football was sublime.
The poor red shirts were overrun
till saved by the clock — half time!

The London manager bustled in
to the visitors' dressing room
and saw the shellshocked Charlton men
bemused and sunk in gloom.
'Lift up your spirits!' he growled,
'There's always the second half!'
But his hopeful words were greeted
with a hollow croaking laugh.
'They've done you a favour, lads,' he said,
'Play soccer? They've taught you how!
'Pass to your own, and keep the ball —
'It's simple, so do it now!'

By God these streetwise Londoners
don't half learn bloody fast —
they grabbed the ball from the kick-off whistle
and passed and passed and passed
and then they booted it up in the air
and headed it round and round
till the Pompey players, in a following flock
jerked heads like birds in a cuckoo clock
and lost all touch with the ground.
The crowd yelled 'Feet!' in grave dismay —
where are the football aristocrats?
What's happened to Pompey's cultured play?
The game's collapsed in disarray.
A man sent off! We could even lose!
How could a triumph end this way?

Backs to the wall
Bring on Aspinall
change shorty Walsh for Lawrence.
Slide, fight, hack
but Charlton attack
wave after wave, in torrents.

We look at our watches, bite our lips
tear up our hopeful betting slips
         feel each slow minute sliding by
like a sharpened blade on skin
         and beg for the final whistle
with a shrill, sad, shrieking din.
At last it came. The players left;
         let's hope they've been admonished.
That swarm of clumsy Cockney drones
         should have been demolished.

RICHARD WILLIAMS

Bird in Hand
(The FA Cup – 1945 to 2008)

We drink in the presence of greatness.
A glorious bird of paradise
that fills the room with life.
Wanderers to Portsmouth all roads between,
a coach trip ride through hedge-screened fields.

This monochrome world that we engraved
as so many lives were sliding past.
Waiting for the blackout to end,
as if nothing we did really mattered,
as if watching was all that there was.

So we taped up all the windows,
made do with any small victory,
turned out the lights and kept quiet.
As the radio spat static and crackled,
keeping our hopes in the dark.

And here we are only nine months on,
a country pub where they kept it safe
for five lost years as the city burned,
payloads emptied on a scrap of earth.
Abide with me and flags at half mast.

Abide with me and a sea of blue.
Wembley stadium and Kanu scores,
forty-something men so close to tears,
my daughters and I in our Pompey shirts.
The final whistle on a perfect day.

And here we are on the journey home,
brilliant colours will fade to none,
as the flags we carry are furled away.
Like Tommy Rowe at ninety-two
leaving all thoughts in the dark.

So drink to the presence of greatness,
for everything you do really matters.
Enjoy all of your victories.
Turn on the lights and sing out,
for living is all that there is.

(The FA Cup spent much of the Second World War at the Bird in Hand pub in Lovedean. It came back to the pub for one night after Portsmouth won the cup in 2008. I sat near John Westwood (Pompey's most famous fan), at the final, and can confirm that he was in tears. (R. W.)

A garrison town

Oh yes, my friend, you know me well,

you've seen me down the DSS

ROBERT HULL

On Portsmouth Station

a policeman
with a gun on his arm

arresting my
leisurely progress.

It flashes into mind
that if I look directly

down the barrel
of his vision

I might awaken the glint
of intent scrutiny,

and this sixty-something,
uncertain-looking

Caucasian male
with a faded rucksack

and the appearance
of being somewhat

abandoned by life, maybe,
or success or a woman

or all three, might seem
to a young man

carrying state-sanctioned
rapid-action hardware

to have been left behind
suspiciously unattended.

Cup of Tea

Oh yes, my friend, you know me well,
You've seen me down the DSS.
A dog and a distinctive smell,
No worldly cares, no fixed address.

You've watched me busking in the street
With questions running round your head:
Which of our lives is more complete?
How do you get your hair to dread?

You wish you had a clearer sense
Of who is better, who is worse.
You eye in frightened innocence
My tattoos, the small child I nurse.

And now you smile, reach for your purse,
Attempt to lower your defence.
I speak no blessing and no curse,
Just 'New Big Issue. One-seventy pence.'

Hilsea Lines

Ramparts on the throat
of this city – a tender-tight thread
separating Portsea Island
from spreading suburbia.

Through this neck
creek and moat compete
for cormorant, shank, egret
and a pair of kingfishers.

A tin-foil sky attempts to keep
the city at absolute body temperature;
but people unwind here,
and find someone other than themselves.

Some boil over –
a fractious sky loosens young men
who erupt as though they have tasted
brackish water of creek and moat.

On the narrow footpath
on top of Victorian ramparts –
built to keep us from the French,
a young man has hanged himself.

The circumstances known only
to the ranger who found him,
and his mother and father, but
the tree is festooned in flowers.

NFP*

Even in the centre of Pompey the sea
air, fresh-blown across acres and acres

of desert-ocean, is salt-sweet. I note
my swelled reflection as I window-shop:

I'm settling here, becoming a Pompey mum,
here where flowers live in concrete council flowerpots.

A boy of three stops beside an opening city bud
and leans towards its orangeness, lips parted.

His mum hits his head: *kinurryup*! and
his face is hitting petals and she is stomping off

and he is running after her, gurning back the tears
and I'm left standing, weeping, like a Pompey freak.

*(NFP: Normal For Portsmouth — local social services shorthand meaning
'intervention not viable')*

Catfight, Kingston Modern, 1963

Outside the secondary modern gate
Persil nets twitch behind Edwardian windows.

A festering grievance reveals itself:
the acned boyfriend tempted away,
nickname too true to bear.

Now the grisly gavotte: a cheek branded,
an inky fistful of backcombed hair, scratches,
sole marks on a white ankle sock.

The protagonists blink tears,
hoick up grey pleated skirts,
shoulder Woolworths satchels, hatch excuses
for a hand-knitted sleeve stretched for ever.
Rubbing bruises, each claims victory.

Ten voyeurs dissolve into the darkening street,
remember the Headmistress's vowels
more suited to a country boarding school:
'Gels who watch these unedifying spectacles
face certain detention.'

(Kingston Modern is now City of Portsmouth Girls' School)

The Tattooed Men of Portsmouth

I am trying to think of the tattooed men of Portsmouth,
who walk, tall as warriors, along the sea front
bearing their dragon-framed bellies from pier
to pier — when the sun is at its height.

Their décor is snakes — coiled, sleeping, or tigers,
a thorny rose and one long sword — held skyward.
Celtic knots shawl shoulders. Their skin is bronze
and they know the sea means business.

I am trying to think of the tattooed men of Portsmouth —
with their sea, stones and armour — on the concrete
foreshore — standing firm — staring seawards
into a world etched on their chests.

I am trying to think of the tattooed men of Portsmouth —
with their sea, stones, armour and re-enforced concrete —
but I keep being drawn back to the signs — Danger!
Slippery Slope! Fast Current! Beware!

MICHAEL HENRY

Southsea Belle

She loosens the throat of her dress
pompoms like Boule de Neige roses,
sets off at a sultry pace:
quick small seducer-of-men steps.

Outside the Admiral
girls with pick 'n' mix hairdos,
girls with Empire State stilettos.
She takes a ferry across the harbour,
lights wanton on the water.

Grey hulks of warships loiter:
Bristol, Coventry, Edinburgh, Belfast,
her points of compass at anchorage.

Each returning mile a millstone:
passing trees that twist and writhe,
the moon wearing thin as a widow's ring.
Alone, her face pale as cuttlebone,
that feeling of film noir she can't escape,
that feeling of a tightening at her throat.

Bristol, Coventry, Edinburgh, Belfast,
her shipping forecast for the morning.

Leopold Street

Outside the Leopold,
ten to eleven, on
a Wednesday night; two men,
younger than me, have left
a girl or two behind
and now insist upon
sharing all their loving
with me. Their singing is
as fresh as mine in the
shower. 'All my loving',
they call, clearly having
drunk, at least, as much as
I have. 'All my loving',
they cry, 'I will send to
you.' I close my eyes and
I am with them, too, as
they hurl the song into
the open windows of
the street. It crosses my mind
to wonder who you are:
not the young man and his
desperately with-it
facial hair, sunglasses
and cigarette, nor the
anonymous other,
but the you to whom they
sing. Are you impressed? Do
you sit with your back to
the front door, hearing
his promises to be
true? Or are you out the
back laughing with your mates?
Are you as unaware
of them as they are of
me? 'Thanks', I say before
crossing the road, 'no, I
really enjoyed that.' They
are taken by surprise.
'Cheers mate', one of them says.

How I lived with the Brigadiers

'The Dance of Words': a happening at Guildhall —
King Crimson, Captain Beefheart, forgotten turns;
some loon leaping, screaming out, 'Cream Buns',
the smell of dope across the auditorium.
Not quite San Francisco, but its here.

Outside this sober-sided building, the sailors
come, the sailors go — it's rumoured when
the US Fleet is in, special trains come down
from London packed with doxies travelling
to meet their Waterloo — but this may not be true.

It is quite fun, they say, in residential halls,
I go there when I can and sometime fall
asleep on some friend's floor. But I'm
in student digs, Salvation Army style, subject
to two Brigadiers, a man, his fearsome wife.

I have a room-mate; in the night he flings himself
about, on one occasion yells out 'Trapped!',
which almost makes me hit the ceiling. Mrs Brigadier
is full of work she names as good but waters milk,
feeds us offal, keeps our coal fire starved of fuel.

Elegy on a Graffito

Along that misnamed Canal Walk
the railway's looming curtain wall
strides parallel, is overlooked
by brutal sixties council blocks.
There, in deliberate two foot
capitals, loaded with purpose
and almost forty years timeworn,
the brush-stroked statement, green on grime:
'WE LOVE THE VIETCONG'.

Before advent of day-glo spray,
before stencils and CCTV,
whose dissenting hand and eye
conspired to frame this risky sutra?
Back, when bovver-booted skinheads
made fearful my own middle-class
teenage long hair and platform soul;
when the message was the message,
not some braggart's frontier tag.

Now crumbly pointing gets rebuilt;
those painted words bricked over,
forgotten fellow travellers.
But no more writing on the walls,
move on. The rest is masonry.

Direct Action Group

*(In 2004 DAG pressure led to the abandonment of a proposal
to house asylum-seekers near Lee-on-The-Solent, Hants)*

They are not being tortured
or interrogated
or ignored
or patronised at the border.

They inhabit
lyric conservatories
and fastidious gardens,
they are in possession
of effulgent garages
and passports
to sailing clubs.

They seem not to believe
they are among those
who are seeking
in words
bird-song
drink
love
hope

asylum this evening
as usual.

Myself

If I met myself at my door
I would beat myself up!
It's not that I hate myself,
yes I do, no I don't, but I do!

I would ask the monster which is myself,
why were you mean to people?

I would then calm down and offer myself
a glass of water and a tissue,
then I would begin on the real issue.

Why do you hate me, why do I hate you?
We have had each other through thick and thin
and will be together till the day we die.

Stand up, get up, let me in,
for it is I who have done the sin
of hating myself.

Why do you hate yourself?
That is for me to know and you to query.
Do you fear me?

The never-ending voice in my head,
the never-leaving friend at my side.
Why have I hated you all these years?
Why have I wasted so many tears?

You have always caused me grief
and always stopped me getting friends,
but we have been together
in the straight and the bends of life.

What am I saying?
The truth is I do not know.
I am myself and you are yourself,
we both like to wander round Fratton,
eat, sleep. We love dogs.
We share the same interests and hobbies
and I will never have as much in common
with anyone
as I will you, myself.

(by a student at Highlands Pupil Referral Unit)

Lover

I am desire, and you are my slave,
I am the substance you'll forever crave,
You think you could never become a disgrace,
And end up a junkie; addicted, a waste.

So you start to inhale one afternoon,
Then take me in your arms very soon.
And once I've entered deep down in your veins,
Your life will never be the same.

You'll need lots of money, as you'll have been told.
For Darling, I am much more expensive than gold.
You'll swindle your mother, without thought or fear,
You'll let your child starve if it gets you the gear.

You'll mug and you'll steal for my venomous charms,
And feel true contentment when I'm in your arms.
The day when you know the monster you've grown,
You'll silently promise to leave me alone.

You'll think that you've got the mystical knack,
Well sweetie, try getting me off your back.
The vomit, the cramps, your guts in a knot,
Your trembling nerves screaming for just one more shot –
Hot sweats, cold chills, the withdrawal pains,
Can only be stopped by those little brown grains.

There's no other way, there's no need to look,
For deep down inside, you'll know when you're hooked.
You'll give up your morals, conscience and heart,
And you will be mine, till death do us part.

The Lodge Diner: 'People not Profits'
(Art in Victoria Park)

Along a good lay-line
It stands on the corner
Brews up coffee so fine
Good seats get you warmer
While being served great food.

Inside exhibitions
If you're in the mood
For artistic visions
As you dine choose your wine,
Beer, water, or Earl Grey.
Mochachino's the line –
Sets me up for the day.

The Precinct Preachers

The Busker:
'Life is like this song,
Life is like this song,
Life is like this song,
Repetitive and pointless.

'I never wanted to be born
Biology would have its way
And when I die, then I'll be dead
I got no soul, I got no say
With all my heart and head
I wish I'd not been born.'

The Evangelist:
'Does your life look futile?
Does your life go nowhere?
Does your life need meaning?
Find the truth in Jesus!

'He is the One, the Three in One
The Son of God, the Son of Man
We celebrate his suffering
The ineradicable stain
Of Sin upon our souls
He bleaches with his blood.'

Unheeded and unheard by all but me,
I take in all their words and chew them well,
And sit, and, passive, listen, hope, and wait.

Ship's Company

Let there always be a way through water

Man to Man

Your divers' bubbling summons has roused
Us at our mooring, where we lay
Waiting for Gabriel.

We are the men who foundered, who plunged
Smartly to our stations, under
The eyes of the bright king

In July weather, in a flat calm,
In home waters, among the fleet,
Without giving reasons.

The long wait spliced us. Artificers,
Officers, gunmen and bowmen,
Old salts, surgeons, sea-cooks,

Captain, Vice-Admiral, all of us
Lay together in our common
Catafalque like lovers.

Tides passed. The mild fish consumed our flesh,
Bones dropping neat and nice as rope coils,
Jaws fell, grinning welcome

To the certain resurrection, when
The lovely rigging of the bone
Leaps to the last whistle

Of Bo'sun Christ. But the next coming
Was yours, who harried our petty
Harvest of every day —

Boots, bricks, barrels, baskets, rigging-blocks,
Dice, daggers, dead-eyes, pipe-and-drum,
A bell, books, candlesticks,

Hairs of the ship's dog, bones of the rat
He might have caught, bones of the men
Embalmed in Solent mud.

What will you do with us, you to whom
The sea yields its secrets, who plumbed
Our permanent instant?

Museums will house our chattels. Even
Degraded wood has its uses.
Only our nameless bones

Remain dully unadaptable,
Impossible to show or sell,
Being the same as yours.

(The Mary Rose, built 1503, served in wars against France, Scotland and Brittany, but sank in the Solent under the eyes of Henry VIII on 19 July 1545. The wreck was salvaged in 1982 in one of the most complex operations of maritime archaeology. Portsmouth's Historic Dockyard now houses the ship and recovered artefacts.)

Majestic Rose

Reborn into the air in a baby-yellow
inflatable, the *Mary Rose* now lies
breech in a new womb, in the pumped
drizzle of a gum-filled rain.
Come into the humid half-light,
and watch the still wood.
Time pulses slowly for the majestic:
twenty-two years to emerge,
and she'll not feel the saline breeze,
the pounding boots, the carpenter's
surgical stroke again. She's stripped bare,
silent as the Solent in winter, as we stare
and will her to surge the surf again.

Mary Rose

It started with a sharp order
splintering across the wooden deck
and the leather-jerkined crew
left steaming guns,
        forgetting the French

and sun winked at sea
as Henry stood on the beach
watched men line up, starboard side

and under their weight the boat bowed
      slowly at first,
           then keeled

as ocean invaded open gun ports
chased across lower decks, tearing
cannons from chains

then sailors jumped into waves
fast as bathers at a holiday park
      despite the watching king

and only a slim black mast
was above water
tilting shoreward, as if still
trying to obey the order to salute.

My Boy Jack

'Have you news of my boy Jack?'
      Not this tide.
'When d'you think that he'll come back?'
      Not with this wind blowing, and this tide.

'Has any one else had word of him?'
      Not this tide.
For what is sunk will hardly swim,
      Not with this wind blowing, and this tide.

'Oh, dear, what comfort can I find?'
      None this tide,
      Nor any tide,
Except he didn't shame his kind
      Not even with that wind blowing, and this tide

Starfish

I'm standing on the glass floor
of Spinnaker Tower
when I take his call,
watching as our six-year-old
lies at my feet
limbs splayed on the glass
a starfish dressed in orange,
mouth pressed against the cold.

They've surfaced within sight of us
and he's standing on the casing
of the submarine.
Him and twenty others
all gabbling 'love you,
love you, love you'
into mobile phones
as the Solent wets their feet.

And I'm never sure
about the curse or the blessing
of these brief communications.
when I know
that many weeks will pass
until he's here and smiling
with me, at the starfish on the glass.

Portsmouth Valentine

Napoleon and Nelson left
women at home to manage or mope.
But Emma danced naked on tables,
and Josephine didn't wash.

I stretch out across the bed,
can sleep landscape if I wish.

In dreams, I am eating soap,
or clearing the deck of spoons,
when I hear your key in the lock,
the ghost of you home
before the ship even docks.

Naval Engagement

At first, lying in bed
back to back
more like enemies
than lovers
as we fire at each other
broadsides of wind
explosions that will
inflict no damage
in chemical warfare
back in our century.
Refusing to pass in the night
our ships turn round.
Now, facing each other,
our arms like grappling irons
love's boarding party
enters in
to claim its prize.

So it's goodbye Nelson,
farewell Lady Hamilton,
as our ships drift apart
on sea's rocking sleep
and the happy sailors
return to their wives
knowing it's love, not war,
that's worth fighting for.

Notes from a Submariner's Diary

We are forty days dived
when I have the coffin dream.
I am boxed in,
air black, lid tight.
I wake up clawing
at Mac's bunk above,
sweating in my sleeping bag,
and struggling to breathe.

We're charting hostile waters,
listening out for threat
and it takes a while
to slow my heart.
While I wait,
I trace the picture
by my bed.

We're in the park at Southsea,
the boys are flying on the swings,
and the amber light
from the winter sun
echoes in my dreams.

Pressed
(after the painting 'Gala Press Gang', Portsmouth Museum)

I thought I saw you at The Walls
      as we slipped out
           with the tide

On my wrist, your ribbon
      until the day
           of my return.

In the smash of the Cape wind
      I hear
           your song

In the eye of the albatross
      see
           your gaze

In the first mate's lash
      feel
           the stroke of your hair

In the water's spray
      taste
           the salt of our loving.

The old sea dog you just might see
if you stays late at GunWharf Quay

He wore an untrained, forked and rum-stained
Grey and grizzled beard
Did the ghost of Captain Sam
An old sea dog was he
Ten rugged lifetimes before the swaying mast
Upon the wild and untamed cold and briny sea

And when the haunting mood was on him
And when the Moon time and tide allowed
Upon the edge of Gun Wharf Quay
He'd dance the sailor's hornpipe, eccentric
And always draw a decent crowd

The wife he never married
The sloe-eyed ghost, the Baltic Tanya
Played careless fiddle for his dancing
And tossed her once lush long black hair
And when the Moon time and tide was right
They'd haul out his dusty squeeze box
And play and dance into the Pompey night

In his one good ear he wore a gold ring
In the ring there hung a bright and shiny key
To a studded chest of buried treasure
Hidden deep, deep beneath the silky shifting sand
In a distant mysterious strange and unmapped land

'There's men gone mad as pancakes in the trying'
Said the ghost of Captain Sam
'Their crumbling bones bleached by the blazing Sun
From Jamaica to Espania'

'And many a Pompey girl left weeping in her lamentations'
Added the sloe-eyed ghost, the Baltic Tanya
'There's pirate gold for the taking
For them as is foolish or brave enough to try'
Said the ghost of Captain Sam
The crowd leaned forward, silenced
The ghost of Captain Sam he stroked his beard
There were those who thought him crazy

There were those who simply stood and stared
'Spanish gold a plenty for those who ain't afeared'
And all moved forward to listen when he lowered his voice
And whispered through his forked and rum stained
Grey and grizzled beard

'They set sail from Old Portsmouth
Them as never afore sailed together
Was the lure of Spanish gold that got em started
In full and straining sail in heavy weather'
And the sloe-eyed ghost, the Baltic Tanya added
Her frozen once ruby red lips a trembling
'I do not think they were very clever men' she smiled
And the ghost of Captain Sam said 'That's right my darling'

'But when the blood is running
And there's treasure to be had
And when the grog is flowing
And once the plan is made
Men will climb the rigging
And scorn the men as stayed
And when the wind is whipping
And when the waves break hard
And when the ship is creaking
And seems about to fall apart
Men will, to a man repent their sins
And implore God into their racing hearts
'Of course' he said 'They were all lost, every one'
All drowned in the wild and untamed cold and briny sea
Tis the reason we stand here afore ye
To tell you this true and terrible story
Of how foolish men can be'

And with that he danced the sailors hornpipe
And the sloe-eyed ghost, the Baltic Tanya
Played fiddle for his dancing
And the crowd they screamed and cheered
As her once lush long black hair took flight
As they played and danced eccentric
Into the Pompey night

Spice Island

Oysters slipped off their tongues, brine summons
potent already, crowds and tide gathering, wind
clearing the sky. Tenderly he watched her hand
freed from the glove, naked and spiced,

hover over each of the shells, their glued backs purple
from the water. She unlocked them with her ivoried knife,
trying to be modest with her ring. They filled
earthenware bowls with their shells' spent silver.

The fleet bulged through the owl-eyed swell of windows.
Fifty taverns roared. Under the whores' broadside
midshipmen trembled and ached. The pinnace was held
to carry the admiral from shingle out to Spithead.

The horizon jostled with sails. Gulls were aloft
like all hands rigging the sky. Sergeants at Arms
sifted Spice Island alleys for powder monkeys.
The port was drained like ale barrels, ragged air

seasoned with display, sample, bargain, handshake:
cinnamon, nutmeg and cloves; caraway, fine
dusts of peppers, coriander; musky oils
seductive among the salts of wind and piss.

Merchants watched with the women the spreading fleet,
the billows of skirts and sails, the large kerchiefs
still waving after the last stern turned the headland.
Gradually the bidding resumed for East Indies cargoes.

From the quarter deck the mainland faded. He held
the glove, remembering the creak of the bed as she turned;
currents and tides, kindlings of oils and spices:
a cry, and her tongue sharpening on his own.

Spithead Review

In eighteen ninety seven,
at Spithead Royal Review,
proceedings were just starting
when *Turbinia* raced through.

A hundred and sixty warships
were anchored row by row,
what was this upstart doing,
showing they were slow?

The man was Charles Parsons,
sixth son of Earl of Rosse,
his turbine just rejected,
the Admiralty's own loss.

A steam launch chased *Turbinia*,
but just confirmed the fact
that all the naval vessels
were too slow to react.

Within fifteen years or so,
warships, and liners too,
were driven by steam turbines,
to plough the ocean blue.

Pompey chimes

Now gather round, I'll tell ye all the sorry tale ...

Dockyard Matey's Sons
(sung in the Portsmouth dockyards)

We're the dockyard mateys' sons
sitting on the dockyard wall,
watching our poor fathers
doin' bugger all.

Soon we'll be older —
we'll be dockyard mateys too,
just like our poor fathers,
with bugger all to do.

The Bumboat woman's story

I'm old, my dears, and shrivelled with age, and work, and grief,
My eyes are gone, and my teeth have been drawn by Time, the Thief!
For terrible sights I've seen, and dangers great I've run
I'm nearly seventy now, and my work is almost done!

Ah! I've been young in my time, and I've played the deuce with men!
I'm speaking of ten years past. I was barely sixty then:
My cheeks were mellow and soft, and my eyes were large and sweet,
POLL PINEAPPLE'S eyes were the standing toast of the Royal Fleet!

A bumboat woman was I, and I faithfully served the ships
With apples and cakes, and fowls, and beer, and halfpenny dips,
And beef for the generous mess, where the officers dine at nights,
And fine fresh peppermint drops for the rollicking midshipmites.

Of all the kind commanders who anchored in Portsmouth Bay,
By far the sweetest of all was kind LIEUTENANT BELAYE.
LIEUTENANT BELAYE commanded the gunboat HOT CROSS BUN,
She was seven and thirty feet in length, and she carried a gun.

With a laudable view of enhancing his country's naval pride,
When people inquired her size, LIEUTENANT BELAYE replied,
'Oh, my ship, my ship is the first of the Hundred and Seventy-ones!'
Which meant her tonnage, but people imagined it meant her guns.

Whenever I went on board he would beckon me down below,
'Come down, Little Buttercup, come' (for he loved to call me so),
And he'd tell of the fights at sea in which he'd taken a part,
And so LIEUTENANT BELAYE won poor POLL PINEAPPLE'S heart!

But at length his orders came, and he said one day, said he,
'I'm ordered to sail with the HOT CROSS BUN to the German Sea.'
And the Portsmouth maidens wept when they learnt the evil day,
For every Portsmouth maid loved good LIEUTENANT BELAYE.

And I went to a back back street, with plenty of cheap cheap shops,
And I bought an oilskin hat and a second-hand suit of slops,
And I went to LIEUTENANT BELAYE (and he never suspected ME!)
And I entered myself as a chap as wanted to go to sea.

We sailed that afternoon at the mystic hour of one —
Remarkably nice young men were the crew of the HOT CROSS BUN,
I'm sorry to say that I've heard that sailors sometimes swear,
But I never yet heard a BUN say anything wrong, I declare.

When Jack Tars meet, they meet with a 'Messmate, ho! What cheer?'
But here, on the HOT CROSS BUN, it was 'How do you do, my dear?'
When Jack Tars growl, I believe they growl with a big big D –
But the strongest oath of the HOT CROSS BUNS was a mild 'Dear me!'

Yet, though they were all well-bred, you could scarcely call them slick:
Whenever a sea was on, they were all extremely sick;
And whenever the weather was calm, and the wind was light and fair,
They spent more time than a sailor should on his back back hair.

BELAYE would admit that his men were of no great use to him,
'But, then,' he would say, 'there is little to do on a gunboat trim
I can hand, and reef, and steer, and fire my big gun too –
And it IS such a treat to sail with a gentle well-bred crew.'

After a fortnight's cruise, we put into port one day,
And off on leave for a week went kind LIEUTENANT BELAYE,
And after a long long week had passed (and it seemed like a life),
LIEUTENANT BELAYE returned to his ship with a fair young wife!

He up, and he says, says he, 'O crew of the HOT CROSS BUN,
Here is the wife of my heart, for the Church has made us one!'
And as he uttered the word, the crew went out of their wits,
And all fell down in so many separate fainting-fits.

And then their hair came down, or off, as the case might be,
And lo! the rest of the crew were simple girls, like me,
Who all had fled from their homes in a sailor's blue array,
To follow the shifting fate of kind LIEUTENANT BELAYE.

That summer afternoon

In wartime England, one July,
Two schoolboy friends of mine and I
Lay deep in meadow grass of rye
       That summer afternoon.

The river Meon close at hand,
Meandered through the lush green land
To join the Solent's sea and sand,
       That summer afternoon.

We joked, and laughed, discussing japes,
And how we wriggled out of scrapes,
The strawberry fields, and swift escapes,
       That summer afternoon.

Then patterning the sky of blue
White vapour trails snaked into view,
Where droning German bombers flew,
       That summer afternoon.

Two fiery Spitfires pecked their tails
Like hungry birds attacking snails,
With tracer bullet coffin nails,
       That summer afternoon.

One crippled bomber, smoked and spun
Away from its pursuer's gun.
The aircrew baled out one by one
       That summer afternoon.

A silken chute was drifting near
To where we lay, and it was clear
The enemy would land by here
       That summer afternoon.

With bated breath we watched him fall
Beyond a flint-built boundary wall,
A silken shroud enveloped all,
       That summer afternoon.

Up the gravelled lane we sped,
First one, and then the other led.
No plan of action in our head,
       That summer afternoon.

The tangled chute in silent rest
Across a hawthorn hedge lay stressed,
Deflated, torn and quite grotesque,
   That summer afternoon.

Two local men with pitchforks armed,
Protective of the land they farmed
Arrived, and scuttled round alarmed,
   That summer afternoon.

They pondered, should the silk be speared
To apprehend an enemy feared,
But then a bright red stain appeared
   That summer afternoon.

And as the silk was dragged aside
We saw a German lad had died
With clear blue eyes still open wide,
   That summer afternoon.

Impaled upon a sharpened stake,
The bloody sight was hard to take.
What gruesome memories war can make
   On summer afternoons.

Based on a real-life incident, c. 1941

The Liner She's a Lady

The Liner she's a lady, an' she never looks nor 'eeds
The Man-o'-War's 'er 'usband, an' 'e gives 'er all she needs;
But, oh, the little cargo-boats, that sail the wet seas roun',
They're just the same as you an' me a-plyin' up an' down!

Plyin' up an' down, Jenny, 'angin' round the Yard,
All the way by Fratton tram down to Portsmouth 'Ard;
Anythin' for business, an' we're growin' old
Plyin' up an' down, Jenny, waitin' in the cold!

The Liner she's a lady by the paint upon 'er face,
An' if she meets an accident they count it sore disgrace:
The Man-o'-War's 'er 'usband, and 'e's always 'andy by,
But, oh, the little cargo-boats! They've got to load or die.

The Liner she's a lady, and 'er route is cut an' dried;
The Man-o'-War's 'er 'usband, an' 'e always keeps beside;
But, oh, the little cargo-boats that 'aven't any man,
They've got to do their business first, and make the most they can!

The Liner she's a lady, and if a war should come,
The Man-o'-War's 'er 'usband, and 'e'd bid 'er stay at home;
But, oh, the little cargo-boats that fill with every tide!
'E'd 'ave to up an' fight for them, for they are England's pride.

The Liner she's a lady, but if she wasn't made,
There still would be the cargo-boats for 'ome an' foreign trade.
The Man-o'-War's 'er 'usband, but if we wasn't 'ere,
'E wouldn't have to fight at all for 'ome an' friends so dear.

'Ome an' friends so dear, Jenny, 'angin' round the Yard,
All the way by Fratton tram down to Portsmouth 'Ard;
Anythin' for business, an' we're growin' old
'Ome an' friends so dear, Jenny, waitin' in the cold!

STUART OLESKER

The Ballad of John Pounds

I'll sing of a cobbler deserving of fame,
The pride of Old Portsea, John Pounds is his name.
All the ragged and hungry our good man enrols
In a shop that's a school for the mending of soles.

See our John in the dockyard – he's cream of the crop,
And only fifteen, why he'll soon reach the top.
But he falls from the dry dock and fractures his thigh
Is it over for him? No – I'll tell you for why.

No more dockyard apprentice – but Fate's not unkind
As he rests for a while he finds food for the mind.
Yes he's hungry for learning – now reading's a treat –
Could this appetite spread to the waifs in the street?

For his nephew, who's lame, special boots he provides
And he teaches him cobbling – but much more besides,
Then the thought comes to John 'Offer learning for free!'
See the magical change in the streets of Portsea!

With a hot baked potato he welcomes the poor.
Though it's nosh that attracts 'em – they're asking for more.
For the poor of Portsea reading, writing abounds
And this free education they owe to John Pounds.

Now behold, a fine portrait of cobbler and class.
From the print and example great things come to pass.
From a cobbler in Portsea in a workshop so small
Grows the Ragged School vision – free learning for all!

*John Pounds (1766-1839), severely injured following a fall in a dockyard accident,
established himself as a cobbler in Portsea, where he became a significant figure in the
Ragged Schools movement. He was gifted teacher, offering free education to poor street
children. Pounds taught reading, arithmetic, cooking, carpentry and shoemaking.*

The tale of Jack the Painter

Now gather round, I'll tell ye all the sorry tale of Jack
Who left his home in Edinburgh to walk the Devil's track,
And how he did the damnedest deeds, creating a sensation,
And boasted of his Yankee plans to terrorise the nation.
Learn why he'll die a ragged flag a-fluttering from a mast
And listen to the speech he makes before he breathes his last:

'Eternal life awaits, they said, if you shun sin and error
But I sought immortality on earth through acts of terror.
I left for London where to make my mark was my intent
But fell among fair-weather friends and soon my wealth was spent.
From painting I could little earn and soon I turned to crime,
Played Burglar, Rake and Highwayman in life's strange pantomime.

'I also played the soldier bold – to gain free food and pay
Enlisting under different names – deserting in a day.
To 'scape the long arm of the law I had to run away
I jumped on board a sailing ship bound for Americay.
From Yankee rebels I learned how to spit on 'Good King George',
Sailed home to England where I hoped firm friendships I would forge.

'I came to Portsmouth where I heard some churchman shared my views
But will he preach mere peace and love – or will he light the fuse?
The fuse I fashioned – fine device – my fiendish bold invention
To set our docks and fleet ablaze – became my sole intention.
But allies – Yankee souls in France and English secret spies
Did let me down or played me false – and I believed their lies.

'There's many a man in government and many a reverend too
Who should be hanging from the mast as I shall shortly do.
No martyrs they, our memories of them will soon grow fainter
But generations hence will know the name of Jack the Painter.'
So boys and girls, when Satan calls, you always must aspire
To highest virtue. Do not stray – and never play with fire!

Jack the Painter (aka James Hill, James Hinde and James Aiken) was a painter in the Portsmouth Dockyard who tried to assist the American colonists in their war against the British Crown. He set fire to dockyards in Portsmouth and Bristol (but failed at Plymouth). He was hanged in Portsmouth from the 64-ft mizzenmast of the Arethusa. Twenty thousand people came to witness the execution.

I'm Tom Ellis Owen
(tune: I'm Burlington Bertie)

I'm Tom Ellis Owen
I've seen Southsea growin'
From village to town to resort.
I've cleaned up a city
Made Southsea quite pretty
Made money from houses you've bought.

I'm Tom, Tom,
Bourgeois Gentilhomme,
But to help the less well off you know;
I build workers' houses –
Respect this arouses:
All part of the Tom Owen show.

Fine buildings I fashion,
It's kind of a passion,
But a terrace called Portland won't sell.
Despite all my trying,
The punters aren't buying;
The reason is simple to tell:

Search, search –
But no nearby church,
That's why they've not bought my abode.
Without hesitation,
I find my salvation
By building St Judes in Kent Road.

Southsea's character was in large part created by Thomas Ellis Owen (1804-63),
architect, builder and developer. He built many elegant houses, as well as St Jude's
Church (which he funded himself) and several – now much sought-after – houses for the
poor. Dovercourt, in Kent Road, now part of Portsmouth High School, was his home.

Odorous Pompey
(tune: Beautiful Dreamer)

There's an aroma
Pungent and strong
Rotting cadavers
And pigs — What a pong!

Beautiful stenches
Float on the breeze
Bringing a promise of lethal disease.

Come visit Pompey
Odorous spot
Home of pollution,
And fish gone to rot
What might await you
When you arrive?
Very slim chances that you will survive.

By the 1840s, Portsmouth's population had grown, and the marshes degenerated into polluted hotbeds of cholera and other diseases. The city's Victorian sewage system, supported by (recently upgraded) pumping stations resolved the sanitation problem.

Convicts on the First Fleet (1717)

Our darlings sailed from Solent shores,
  Haul away, haul away,
condemned to serve a convict's term,
  Haul away; haul away.

The fleet they're in's the first to go,
across the world to Holland Land,

Its human cargo's misery
is matched by hardship and disease,

For seas are cruel and winds cut keen,
few mourn the lot of prison wretch,

When Magistrates pass sentence harsh,
on crime that poverty imposed,

All common folk are powerless,
when Rich claims Right, and Weak ill-wronged,

Years do not change the human heart,
though fleets may sail the Poor remain,

No argosy relieves their plight,
Humanity's a Ship of Fools,

   Haul away; haul away.

The chorus, 'Haul away; haul away' follows each line of the solo

Heave away my Johnny
(A rope hauliers' shanty)

As I was going out one day, down by Clarence Dock
        Heave away, my Johnny, heave away
I heard a would-be emigrant talking to Tap Scott
        Hand away, my jolly boys, we're all bound to go.

'Good morning, Mr Tap Scott.' 'Good morning, sir,' he say,
'Have you got good sailing ships bound for Amerikey?'

'Oh yes, I have got packet-ships. I've got one or two;
'I've got the Josey Walker, besides the Mary Lou.'

'You take the Josey Walker, and tomorrow she will sail,
'With some four hundred emigrants, and a thousand bags o' mail.'

Deep down in my pockets, I had saved up all my pay,
so I headed for the dockyard, and for fine Amerikay.

But now I'm lost in Washington, and I'm creeping through the street,
Without a penny in my pockets and not a crust to eat.'

I spit on Josey Walker and the day that she set sail!
For them Yankees robbed me blind and then threw me into jail.

The chorus lines follow each line of solo, as shown in the first stanza.
Tap Scot was an emigration agent

Handy Jim
(A Portsmouth rope-hauling shanty)

I courted a girl named Sally Jane,
        So handy, me boys, so handy.
Sally Jane was a kitchen maid,
And often to her kitchen I strayed,
To find me a dish of something hot.

But one fine night, through my bad luck,
The missus came home – in the copper I got.
But the missus had come the clothes for to wash.
The fire being lit, the copper got hot,

And the missus she came to stir up the pot,
And out I jumped, all smoking hot,
The missus she fainted and cried 'Stop thief!'
But I was out like a gun got shot.

When the missus came to – oh what a fuss!
Poor Sally, she got the sack that day.
Then she came to me and said straightway –
'I've lost my character, place likewise.'

Says I, 'My dear, now never you mind,
Next Sunday morn' we'll go and get wed' –
But Sunday morn' I went to sea instead.

So now, my boys, when courting you go,
If the missus turns up, in the copper don't stow,
If you're handy there, you're handier here.
One more pull, and up steady and slow –
The mate cries 'Belay!' so down we will go.

The chorus: 'so handy, me boys, so handy' follows each line of the solo

The lonely city

...there are many oceans between us now

Gripped

I sat on the wall
by the shuttered
ice cream kiosk

To watch the huge balloon
that had settled
on the horizon

Its tail of crimson light
trailed like a ragged ribbon
across the surface of the sea

I held on until
all that was left
was a cuticle of red

Then I let go
and walked away
as if it was nothing

St James's Hospital

Again I leave the ward and look out through
the windscreen at the bluebells on the grass,
again see Sister's eyes. She'd thought I knew

that if you went home it would be to pass
your last few weeks with him. It would be sad
to separate them, she said in that glass

cubicle with its desk and stubby pad
of death certificates. It would be cruel
too, hopeless as he seems to have been, Dad,

at coping as she put it. But you, you'll...
won't you? I'll what? I nodded though. Yes, I....
Bluebells like bluebells in the woods at school.

And then from Fratton Park a massive sigh
filling the clouds and draining down the sky.

How little is left

> winter dusk
> how little is left of the moon
> how lovely it is

Getting older now, feeling vulnerable after my operation, weak as a kitten, I refuse to accept – as I refused when I lost you – that suffering is wanting it not to be so, that I wouldn't hurt like this if I surfed the convalescence, the grief. I need pain.

The sea churned all day and gulls cowered on the Common.

> after a gale
> kelp-stink in the moonlight,
> crashing waves

With a stick, I can shuffle along the seafront after dark and start to think of something other than me. Recovering now, I recall those games we won together, what a partner you were.

My favourite people are gone from me, which leaves the night, the stars, and the flirty moon winking from wisps of smoke.

> long cold night
> the silver river on the sea
> flows sideways

It is a long night and no sleep. I have to bring you to mind, and put you away again and, in the end, you're mixed up with others in scenes fading to fragments until bits loop stupidly and then I'm bored awake.

> before dawn
> the reflection of dawn
> on the restless sea

Desiderata
(at Langstone Harbour)

New Year's Day comes full of reversal.
The sky has leached colour from the sea,
A wayward moon ghosting the day.

On my tongue flakes of ice,
Forget the first winter of awareness
When snow touched me like this,

Will never forget when I kissed you
For the last time, just as now,
On my lips your frost and snow.

From the pontoon we pour you,
Powdered like snow, into the water.
The pale sea claims you like a lover,

The breeze lifts you into blizzard,
We wait while cold seeps into bone
While our words make the occasion.

You melt in the harbour like those crystals
On my tongue; I wait to leave until
The tide turns with all its ancient ritual.

Pompey Chimes

I wish I could have comforted you more.
but whatever I say: that deaths
are the punctuation marks of history
or there's no such thing as a late night
when you burn the candle at only one end
I hear your sharp voice expostulate.

Instead of reading, we should have sung a wake
and held karaoke hands
as we watched the ashes scatter like grace notes.
We should have quilled something beautiful
in the concealing modesty of Greek.

It was cold on that spit of pontoon
and it seemed to go on for so long
waiting for an appropriate windfall.
But we felt the flow that flows for ages
and I've never seen the sea so luminescent

or such a beautiful blue Dresden sky
as if somehow the painter had painted it wrong.
On land we might have seen his footprints in the grass
but here, although the ashes were cold,
I half-expected to see one of those jets of steam
in the streets of New York rise up out of the sea.

Horizon

At a head-stroke
you sail along sound waves
throat-ravelling to some
rainbow's end in your
voice-box-boat.

We calibrate vibrations
in Hertz. At 25 – 50,
the frequency of purrs:
the same tremor of mending
for muscles, bone, tendon:
for relief of pain.

Come, travel again.

Unfinished Poems for a Friend
(Heather Hart 1962 – 22 December 2009)

Word is saving Heather Hart.
Heather Hart, who could not be saved:
a name on a file, saved to virtual memory,
a memory stick, a removable device.
          I sit at my desk rushing her poems
in time for Monday's funeral
all the sun and moon of her words
ushered into the pages of a flimsy book.

Save to read, read and save:
In Memory of Heather Hart
who would not be saved,
who sailed mid-winter into the wind
in a little voice-box-boat of her own making.
Save as: Unfinished Poem for a Friend

Sally Port
(for Emily)

I remember when all our mornings
were a week long –
when we walked the shore,
counting polar bears in the clouds;
white flapping seagulls fanning the air,
sun winking on water
as we looked across to Gosport,
saw the Lego flats and the ships' masts
porcupining the sky.

I remember, I told her,
how the harbour master was playing boats.
The churn of the Gosport Ferry
the car ferry fizzling to France,
the wash whacking the hot walls,
cleaning the glinting, green ribbons
of seaweed. A small white craft
smoothing through the deep
and the red and black fisherman's smack trawling;
and how we watched the skipper's daughters*
swimming ashore and waved to the passengers
on the Fast Cat day-tripping to Ryde,
while in the dock, the HMSs,
the silent fleet, crouched like sombre monsters
along the water's edge.

One clap of pigeons scuppers my dreams,
of her childhood.

There are many oceans between us now,
and my mornings, my mornings are shorter.
on the way home I stop to read the words –
Let there always be a way through water.

Skippers daughters': white-topped waves

Exiled in the City
(for the Millard sisters, on leaving the Norfolk Fens for Portsmouth)

Rich in delights, this town has small delight:
Incurious grief sighs for lost skies, lost roses,
Wind-gadding nettles, the stream, the heron's flight,
Bright moon, long field-roads whitening as night closes,
And Russian swans, cleaving sub-Arctic air
For Welney's marsh. Here, Spinnaker discloses
It's three red flowers each dusk, whose metal stare
I stare at, and the clouds' grey-purple line
From this high window of a house not mine.

Great Dickens' Portsmouth – and it's dull to me!
Not even charming Austen lures my mind
From doves on the great wind-swayed willow-tree,
Bright dandelions, sparse roses in the wind
Shaken, far in lost Norfolk: rolled away
Dense mist-banks, where no venturing love can find
Even their conjured ghosts, blanked out at day.
Sweet maidens, if these sorrow-stumbling rhymes
Excite your smiles, you'll smile at me sometimes.

Langtone Harbour

On 7th November 1991 my father died. I walked by the shores of Langstone Harbour.

> winter wind —
> two geese turn
> a broad descending circle
> and end
> facing it
> knowing how to touch down
> lightly

At the wake my sons looked after me sweetly, talked of family memories and had me laughing. I returned to Langstone Harbour and watched the birds, and watched yachts on their moorings as fishing boats motored by.

> I lift, judder
> spin and settle
> in your wake
>
> water in the bay
> no trace
> of the splashy wing beats
>
> low tide mudflats —
> I breathe out
> tremble
>
> dense cloud
> the colour of ashes
> the sky is my father

One night, fascinated by the waves slopping inside a wreck with the life-force of the ocean:

> between the ribs
> of the broken boat
> rises the moonlit tide

In the New Year:

> bright cold morning —
> for breakfast let's open
> the last of his marmalade

On the anniversary of his death I stood on the ferry pontoon at Eastney Point, tasting the windblown spray:

> grief, and breathing
> the salty fragrance
> of the deep tide drift

I revisited the Heath by the family home, where we scattered his remains:

> under my foot
> at every step
> my father's ashes

I inherited a dusty oil portrait of my father reading a book, painted in the forties, with a rip in the corner, and I commissioned a friend of mine who is a conservator to repair it, clean it and frame it.

> his portrait restored —
> my father
> younger than me

Winston Churchill Avenue

From my pocket, I took a pen and
three sets of keys:
one ring for work,
one ring for home,
one ring that I will soon return;
a handkerchief,
a list of children – cheerful faces
clapping Cinderella in the dark
as lights curve colours through the gloom –
a pair of glasses in a case
to replace the lenses in my eyes.

They will sting tomorrow morning
when the curry, the kebab, the chips
and the pizza, the garlic bread and
the burger from a roadside van,
and the beer, the pints of beer,
repeat and burn the back of my throat.

If only I could vomit
and wipe off the shame
of what you have chalked upon
the cell door: my name.

Seventy-five mile drive from London

You've got to drive back of course. Not so good after you've spent the afternoon near Portsmouth Harbour. By the bandstand listening to 'The Red Stripes'. Watching Southsea come alive to dance. Barbecues, semi-naked men and women. Tattoos that I've never seen the like of before. The names of two women encircled one man's nipples. Rose and Sandy. I wondered if they knew each other. Red Stripe himself stomps at the boogie piano. One woman danced by herself. Mesmerised me. The way she pointed her toe. A white shoe moving in time to the trilby perched on her head. She danced all afternoon. Didn't talk to anyone. Threw herself into the last number. Walked off alone. Past the candy floss, fudge stalls. Past the so-called home-made ice cream. Head looking at the ground. Ships sailed out of the harbour.

> sun rises over Hayling
> sinks over Gosport
> all that lies in between

Seaside Town

I sit with a bag of chips on a peeling bench.
Couples chat and gaze at the sea, joggers drape
wires from their ears. My concrete shelter is crumbling.

Across the park, children clamber on climbing frames
and mothers chat. I pour oxtail soup from my flask.
Teenagers play football loudly. I nearly get hit.

On Commercial Road, shoppers stride hurriedly, returning
to their shifts, partners, parents. I light a cigarette, watch
the waterless fountain and go home.

Last Thoughts from Farlington Marshes

The grainy doggy smell of rain
On parched land kissed my lips
My feet plunged into watery aromas
Leaking like escaping spirits meeting
The heavy heaven-scented boughs.

Warm winds lift the crunch of soaked grass
I stop and gaze across the grey estuarine flats
To where a moon weaves a wedge of silvery shadow
Within dark whispering waters.
My focus changes from feet to afar
And my ears meet a wall of birdsound.

No doubting the place; a ley line of winterdew.
I dug with a trowel until the dawn spawned its
Life across the bay sending sounds to a grey blue hue
And chased away all but darkest shadow.
I buried my mind and made good the plot.

If I could have arranged it so that
Your muzzle could rest on my arm
Under the mud it would have been so;
But you were alive and I dead —
And this theatre of abstraction is now closed.
Though you sniff little one you will soon forget
Or else you will never find me.

Looking back

All my yesterdays packed inside me

Marigolds

South-easterly corner of Portsea Isle
windswept open expanse
of stony beach

Treasures hidden
with a star
the brooding skeletons of war –

The Glory Hole
Fraser Range
Fort Cumberland –

Yet the sunset rays
cross the crashing waves
and marigolds grow unexpectedly.

Portsmouth

I remember this town
by the decaying piles of wood on the deserted quays,
by the slack-lipped pallid women,
and the humourless latrinary obscenities.

Love is mechanical here,
worshipped in sticky cinematic cuddles,
by brutish gestures in shop doorways, and under arches
where the old whore flaunts; the cripple huddles.

People are all walking in circles,
their villas a wilderness of anonymity;
northwards the bright lights, the flickering dance halls,
southwards, the grey corrugations of the sea.

To the east lie the merchants and their bankers,
and cringing upon the fringes of respectability
a multitude shrinking from the omniscient historical embrace;
yet, as Auden observed, some of these people are somehow
       happy.

After the bombing in the Second World War

Journey
(The Coventry Cross, Royal Naval Museum, Portsmouth)

I wonder what the blacksmith
would say if he knew the journey
we would take:

forged in medieval times,
iron nails to skew the roof beams
of Coventry Cathedral;

blown apart by German bombs
in 1940 – three relics
rescued from the rubble,

fashioned into a cross,
given to *HMS Coventry,*
sunk in San Carlos water

by Argentine jets
in the Falklands War.
Raised from the seabed,

now displayed in a glass case,
inscription on the plinth
still shining –

'Father forgive them.'

Company of Flowers
(Sinking of The Hood, 24th May 1941)

One late May, this empty jug
up on the shelf was brimful with flowers.
It was wartime — nineteen forty-one —
and filching flowers from woods not a crime.

That day, I went with the other grass widows
bluebelling 'to take our minds from our men'.
Scooping up armfuls to ease our aching hearts
we bathed in oceans of wild hyacinths.

Every vase and jar I could lay hands on
was filled with the fresh and fragrant stems;
this special wedding vessel held the most,
stood in pride of place near the wireless.

At nine, next morning, when I tuned for news
and heard that *Bismarck* had fired her fatal broadside,
that *Hood* had been blown to bits
with fears of few survivors.

I wanted to dash and smash that jug to shards.
Instead I snatched the dead and draggled blooms,
white-stemmed and wrenched from earth, ran
tossing them on the compost heap to rot.

Three days later the news hit home.
In the final chase *Bismarck* had been struck,
ducked under a watery counterpane.
That night in bed I cried for German wives

and wished for a ribbon of bluebells
to circle the earth, a symbol of constancy.
Now, every May reminds me that
this jug deserves the company of flowers.

Emma Hamilton speaks
(Inspired by a plaster cast of Lady Hamilton's hand)

Take me back
to the place where he sleeps,
the swinging cot on *Victory* –
made to measure like a coffin.

Let my hands

re-arrange the white drapes I made;
examine every feathered stitch
worked for his comfort,
count the embroidered flowers
on his coverlet.

Let me know
that something of me
will always touch him.

Troopin'

Troopin', troopin', troopin' to the sea:
'Ere's September come again – the six-year men are free.
O leave the dead behind us, for they cannot come away
To where the ship's a-coalin' up that takes us 'ome today.

> (Chorus)
> We're goin' 'ome, we're goin' 'ome,
> Our ship is at the shore,
> An' you must pack your 'aversack,
> For we won't come back no more.
> Ho, don't you grieve for me,
> My lovely Mary-Ann,
> For I'll marry you yit on a fourp'ny bit
> As a time-expired man.

The Malabar's in 'arbour with the Jumner at 'er tail,
An' the time-expired's waitin' of 'is orders for to sail.
Ho! the weary waitin' when on Khyber 'ills we lay,
But the time-expired's waitin' of 'is orders 'ome to-day.

They'll turn us out at Portsmouth wharf in cold an' wet an' rain,
All wearin' Injian cotton kit, but we will not complain;
They'll kill us of pneumonia – for that's their little way –
But damn the chills and fever, men, we're goin' 'ome to-day!

Troopin', troopin', winter's round again!
See the new draf's pourin' in for the old campaign;
Ho, you poor recruities, but you've got to earn your pay –
What's the last from Lunnon, lads? We're goin' there to-day.

Troopin', troopin', give another cheer --
'Ere's to English women an' a quart of English beer.
The Colonel an' the regiment an' all who've got to stay,
Gawd's mercy strike 'em gentle – Whoop! we're goin' 'ome today.

The Chorus follows each stanza

Victoria

A century stood static, stone below
our cast brass feet as time flies past
in flocks of feathered change. It's cold
in winter, when the morning sun is low
and we are all alone. No Albert here
to keep us company, as we maintain
a hundred years of vigil over this
the city whence our navy ruled the waves.

The heavy Hall across the square from us
is not the first. The first was lost, destroyed
by blasting bombs Brunel could not have dreamed
would be. The deaths, the massive human cost
could even touch a statue, bring us grief.
They moved us, built a new square underneath,
a new Guildhall and so much more besides
as Portsmouth licked its wounds and slowly healed.

The shifting face of England, many-hued,
displays itself before us, as elsewhere
no doubt. Few sailors now carouse and shout,
replaced by youths from all across the globe.
We've seen the faces and the fashions change,
the hems of skirts that rose and fell like ships
upon the turning tide, in cyclic ways
but somehow always fresh and always new.

We understand our people better, now
we've stood and watched the fragments of their lives
played out before our massive metal form.
It seems, these days, a freedom is the norm
that would have irked Our Majesty, back then.
We've watched the years go by in happiness
and sadness and remembrance for the dead;
seen festivals and concerts, dances too,

the workers and the shoppers and the lost,
memorials to what the past has cost,
smiles and frowns and silence, violence and
the strangest little moments of pure joy.
But, tell the truth, the days blur into one —
it's only hindsight splits them into bits.
Most times we're just content to stand and wait,
to shrug away the pigeons with a thought.

Statue of Queen Victoria, Guildhall Square

BROADSHEET BALLAD (1874, Anon)

The Glorious Battle of Southsea

Come list to me, a tale I'll tell
About a battle fought so well,
The sad disaster that befell
      At the glorious battle of Southsea
Now the parson too and the little Jew,
The white mushroom, and the rest of the crew,
Had made up their minds the public to do,
And to line their greedy pockets too,
So they schemed so sly, and so slyly schemed,
While the stupid council slept and dreamed,
And for a time it really seemed
      There'd be no battle at Southsea.

The people's blood began to boil,
When they saw the robbery of the soil,
The free-right of the sons of toil,
      The public highway at Southsea.
So with axe and hammer they cut and slashed,
And the mighty barrier they hacked and gashed,
With battering rams they broke and smashed
      The Company's barrier at Southsea.
Jepsey and Barney and all concerned,
Soon on the Company the tables turned,
With some penny-royal the thing was burned
      Upon the Beach at Southsea.

Now the following night the mushroom thought
That the public should have a lesson taught
So with great array their force they brought,
      Upon the Pier at Southsea
So sticks and bludgeons were handed round,
And the fire engine was on the ground,
To cool the courage of those around
      The Company's Pier at Southsea.
And soon also with this array,
The mushroom man brought on the fray,
And then there was the devil to pay,
      At the glorious battle of Southsea

Now a duce of a stew they all got in,
When they found they were punished for their sin,

So the Bobbies were sent for to stop the din,
        Round the Company's Pier at Southsea.
The little Jew ran home in fright,
The mushroom turned a deathly white,
When they found they'd rais'd a serious fight,
        Round the Company's Pier at Southsea.
Brickbats and stones in showers flew,
And heads and shins were broken too,
The Mayor and the super were in a stew,
        In the glorious battle of Southsea.

Next night a thousand 'specials' came,
All sworn to conquer or die game,
The porters too all swore the same,
        On the Company's Pier at Southsea.
The Mayor read the Riot Act,
And 'ere the Pier had been attack'd,
The soldiers came and the people backed,
        From the Company's Pier at Southsea.
The populace now had had their fill,
With the gallant Ninth' they'd no ill-will,
So they left in charge, and may be still,
        Of the Company's Pier at Southsea.

Three cheers for the Queen and her noble sons,
And all the other Royal guns,
Especially their little ones,
        Now the battle's o'er at Southsea.

GOD SAVE THE QUEEN

In 1861, the first Clarence Pier was opened, charging one penny admission. Several years later, the company erected a barrier across the esplanade to stop the hoi polloi mingling with the Pier's customers. After a protest meeting, a crowd attacked the pier, burning facilities and stoning 30 policemen. The police retaliated and a riot developed. The crowd dispersed when the army was called in and heavy rain fell.

Note on the 'villains' in this ballad: A 'mushroom man' was someone who would pop up, like a mushroom, at the chance of making a quick profit. The 'little Jew' refers to Emmanuel Emmanuel, city leader, mayor and reformer. Emmanuel was instrumental in draining the marshy common, building the esplanade, securing Victoria Park for the public, providing gas, water and drainage, and bringing the railway to Portsmouth. (See his memorial at Canoe Lake.)

Descriptions of Jews — or anyone who could be seen as 'other' — in offensive terms were common in broadsheet ballads.

The Mud Larkers

The skinny-ribbed slum kinds stand knee deep in black oozing mud,
their bodies streaked with the vomit of the sea.

Slithery seaweed, dead crabs, drowned cats, rubber tyres, jagged tins and
broken bottles – the platform for a display.

The smelly, squelching, sucking quagmire holds no fear for these children as
with frenzied fingers they grovel and claw for the farthing slowly sinking
in the slime.

They fight their brothers, like hungry tigers over meat for, should the money
disappear, they will not eat tonight.

From the bridge to the Harbour Station and Gosport Ferry pontoon the
passengers throw coins down into the mud in response to the
Mud Larker's ditty:

> Here you are Gov –
> Throw a penny in the mud
> Penny or two won't break ya!
> Stand on me 'ead for a tanner
> Roll in it for a crown.

When dusk descends and the crowds disappear, they bathe in the incoming
tide; grimy faces washed white again

Babies, pacified by sugar tied in rag, asleep in prams wedged in pebbles on the
shore, are gathered by their older siblings and pushed back home

Pennies rattling in rusty tins means faggots and peas for supper. But this
pleasure is not for long

Tomorrow, with arms outstretched, their begging begins again:
the Mud Larkers' plea echoing across the Harbour

> We love ya lady, we love ya lady
> We love ya money the best
> all that rusty silver
> Roll over for a crown.

See the Mudlarker memorial statue at The Hard.

DAVID COWARD

The Totter's Tale

Listen, Listen can you hear
the Totterman calling loud and clear?
'Ragbones, Ragbones, woollies and jars',
as he drives his horse
round the town's first cars.
Rabbit skins, wild ones, tame ones too,
he'll buy them all for a bob or two.
Calling and travelling street to street
passing bobbies pounding their beat.

Up through Fratton on to North End
Rudmore Cellars on the sharp bend,
back to Portsea through Guildhall Square
passing the lions still sleeping there.
Ladies on corners, they all hear his cry.
He touches his cap
and winks them an eye.
'How much for this lot?' one lady said
smoking a fag and scratching her head.

Caff on the corner. He stops for a brew,
and a warm smile from the cronies he knew
These were the ways of the old Portsmouth pals,
laughing and joking
and telling their tales.
One in the corner caressing a pup,
another one talks of the '39 Cup.
Outside the window, the rain starts to fall
on goes the totter making his call.

Travelling on, the rain on his back
he covers his shoulders
with an old sugar sack.
Odd-coloured horse's head hanging low
pulling the trolley in wind, rain and snow.
There's a living out there, out on the street –
proud of his Portsmouth and the people he meets.
Totterman, Totterman, those long years were kind
left you with memories to light up your mind.

*David Coward writes: The Totterman of this poem is George Seymour, of Woodland Street,
Fratton, my grandfather.*

The pawnshop door
(exhibit 253 Portsmouth Museum)

Wednesdays
when the bread ran out
when she was fed up scraping ha-pennies,
she'd brazen out the shame of the queue,
take pots and pans, crockery,
sheets, an old Sunday suit
and once her wedding ring –
anything that would fetch
a few shillings,
to stand before that painted green door
with the gold letters
PLATE WATCHES JEWELLERY –
the door that haunted her.

The broker,
no kindness in his eyes,
no smile, dead-headed the women
as they came through.
She knew she would get just enough
to tide her over;
enough for fresh milk
and clutching the coppers
he counted into her hand,
pocketing the pawn ticket,
she gathered her children –
passed through the portal of the poor.
The door that haunted her.

LYNDA O'NEILL

Dinnertime

The klaxon sounds at noon
and they stream in two shoals,
eighteen inches apart on sit-up-and-beg Raleighs
through the Dockyard Gates into Queen Street
or past The Keppel's Head, the tattoo parlour.
They see a dozen gap-toothed Mudlarks
up to their grey flannel shorts in sludge,
scrabbling for coppers, the gleam of a sixpence.

Peaked caps over short-back-and-sides,
wide trousers cycle-clipped to their ankles,
their grubby macs flap in the Solent wind.

Like salmon, they push upstream to
Fratton or Southsea, the far reaches of Copnor,
glad not to be unsnapping an Oxo tin of
cheese and Branston sarnies like their mates from
Hilsea or Paulsgrove, too far to cycle home.

Stomachs gnaw on a memory of the breakfast fry-up;
they salivate for Shepherd's Pie
or yesterday's beef, cold today with Piccalilli,
bubble and squeak fried in dripping,
then apple crumble and Birds custard,
a mug of Co-op Ninety-nine.

They swerve in formation onto Commercial Road,
fuelled by the waft of steak and kidney from doorways.
These plumbers, coppersmiths, chippies and sparks
pedal inexorably towards a pension
after the apprenticeship Dad said
would set them up for life.

Cabs

Six cabs or maybe eight,
> Would wait at Fratton Station gate.
All old and slightly seedy,
> With cabbies often somewhat needy,
Sitting on the kerb to gaze,
> At bubbling tar prickling in the haze,
At the nags waiting there
> For a train to bring a fare.

Cabbies weatherbeaten, cabbies old
> What tales they could have told:
Some drinking railway tea,
> Most sitting silent, so it seemed to me.
Perched up on their hard high seat,
> An old rug across the knee.
Had some once been stage coach men,
> Or troopers of the Queen's Cavalry?
Had they fought in distant wars –
> Long past, now merely history?

Then one summer, and I think this weird –
> Like the conjurer with the lady –
They all just disappeared.
> I thought in youthful ignorance,
That they slowly would retire,
> If there were six this summer,
Next there would be five for hire.

I hoped that one last Hackney Cab
> At least would linger still,
As long as the Whitsun Fair
> Was held on Portsdown Hill.
Perhaps I'll ride in one again,
> Ride proudly through the sky
At the final curtain call
> When I say my last goodbye.

Where are they now?

They were the men who sailed the sea,
the crew of the good ship *Victory*.
Jolly tars in Hearts of Oak,
pressed men and gentlefolk.

They sailed out across Biscay,
leaving the quay at old Pompey.
'England expects' said the flags,
for good men and for all those lags.

Ill fed, ill housed but better than ashore,
bullied, flogged, shot at and more.
Weevily biscuits, rum to keep out cold,
we wonder how they could be bold.

Who are their sons in the present day?
Where do they work? Where do they play?
Does the whole city follow the team?
Have they realised their dream?

The goal back then was beat old Boney.
Now they sell Nokia and Sony,
sit at desks, stare at screens.
Do they wonder what all this means?

Places

Shamelessly, the city undressed itself

Haiku

mist clings in the valley,
a steamed-up glass
the rustling trees appear through,
stilled and dripping

Hugh Dunkerley

sound of dance music
the last fishing boat
throbs into place

George Marsh

fresh on the air
over the derelict street:
the scents of fish

Connaire Kensit

like a cine film
the train moves through the city
black white, white black, black …

Sally Mills

from the black sea
a ferry moves into port —
adding lights to lights

Sally Mills

in a Southsea garden
while the neighbours sleep
a fullmoon magnolia

George Marsh

from the hilltop
gazing down on the city —
distant moon

Molly Goulden

after cathedral bells
filling the silence
a west wind roar

Martin Lucas

Where Nan Lived

Linen sheets billow and pistol-crack
on the high line in the country garden
behind her narrow city house.
We go to Marmion Road for
duck eggs, cockles,
cream horns crusted with sugar,
squishing meringues.
Smell the shop that grinds coffee
for old girls in fox pelts set with glass eyes.
Their Edwardian voices speak of better days.

We sit in the street; Nan shucks peas
or polishes uncle's shoes,
teaches me to cast on with big needles.
Turbaned women queue at the pub
with pint jugs for their men.

The rough boys' posse advances;
snakehead belts on short trousers,
scab-lumped knees, gravy chins.
We hear the tinkle of glass.

Soon, wrecking balls
like giant conkers on ropes.
An ASDA stands their now,
not a flat-fronted slice of house
with three wee downstairs rooms,
that slippy linoed passage,
scullery with sodden Blue Bags
on a wooden drainer.

Chelsea Road

Some Sundays the Salvation Army
strikes up in the road outside the house,
The Old Rugged Cross breaches my dreams
as I lie in bed still as a toad.
I don't believe in God, but I believe in sin
the music stirs me into guilt.
I get up and peer through the curtains,
I should dress, go down, put money in the tin.
But I don't, and no-one else does either.
I think of my neighbours tucked up in bed.
Doing and not doing is what beings do,
some with a poem, some with a hymn,
some with a canon of convincing words,
some with just one, slight as amen.

Portsdown Hill

It seemed like miles.
We marched bravely behind you,
foot-soldiers, going in to battle.
Into the evening warmth we trudged
tired but on target.

Uphill manoeuvres,
posting a guard, on the watch for
       fireflies

              glow-worms –
eerie lights –
just a ghost of a chance.
Your summer skirts flapped
like a loose pennant
picked and flicked at by an unseen hand

Your skin scented with hints
of attar of roses
       meadowsweet
            wild strawberries.

At last just as the soft light faded
we gained the top
marked out our positions with hushed voices.
One by one the creatures lit up.
You said they were far off campfires

hinted at the Fort behind us.
Well worth the walk
      the watch
         the wait

I walk alone to this same rendezvous,
sit watching as night falls.
Now my clothes are touched by that same unseen hand.
Just as they used to little lights glow
eyes in the night, flickeringly alive.

I reflect on things that do not seem to change.
The glinting ghosts are worth the wait –
only, without you,
      gleam like
         new stars.

(from) A Sheltered Upbringing

With brick red faces glinting in the sun
forts punctuate the ridge above the hospital,
hunched shoulders on the skyline hidden under grass.
Their narrow eyes are slits for firing on fixed lines.
The gatehouse mouth is open wide:
drill sergeants' frenzy of command,
the clash of rifles in arms drill,
the clump of marching feet
on echoing tarmac, grated on by heels.
A limp flag flutters on a pole.
The sentry grumbles in his box.
The faces of the forts perspire.
They are toy forts, the soldiers lead
that will melt down or have their heads
snapped off, played with by time
and shrunken into distances
a child won't see so far below.
Bugles haul down the sun at last
that dips below the ridge
where lights will twinkle up among the stars.
The irony of forts
that look down on a hospital
and on my father's shellshock cases in the wards:
a child's hand cut by metal toys;
war wounded bleeding to slow death
from memories.

*Queen Alexandra Hospital and the Portsdown Hill forts (Fareham, Wallington, Nelson,
Southwick, Widley and Purbrook)*

Flightless Saucer

Remember?
Close Encounters of the Third Kind
the final scene,
the blackness of the mountain, the silence.

The fantastic array of lights hovering;
arteries of brilliance pulsing
radiating energy, throbbing beacons,
tiny flashes dancing and darting.

Portsdown Hill, the Lookout Point,
survey the scene,
the blackness of the sky to the horizon.

Invert it, turn it over in your mind,
the startling display of light unfurled,
radiant ribbons trailing
through and around, binding and grounding.

An upturned ship, a flightless saucer
brimming with creatures
waiting to flip and soar away.
Remember.

Resurrection Day on Milton Common

The Common wasn't always so
and that's the beauty of it all.

A rubbish tip some thirty years ago,
I still recall the day I sought some peace
to write an essay. Watching lorries
dump their loads instead, I dozed away the hours,
waking just in time to rush for tea.

Now overgrown with brambles, teasels, broom,
it's rats and rabbits that replace the trucks,
the willow grove become a refuge for both wild and tame.
As Labradors and Pointers roam,
you'd never think that inches down
a city's waste has found its rotting, rusting home.

I have a dream sometimes
that on that final Resurrection Day,
as tombstones split and graves erupt,
this former tip will vomit up
a million plastic bags,
some lorries made in '65,
whole legions of fine cycles, BSAs with Sturmey Archers,
tinkling bells, a hundred kitchen sinks,
with gleaming ranks of thermoses
and perfect polished kettles,
Frigidaires and Hoovers, just like new.

And in amongst them all, I pray,
refilled and anxious to be used,
the fountain pen I lost that day.

The Landport Gate

Showing its backside to the modern world
it faces an expanse of neatly mown green
where battles are enacted and polished leather hurled.

The proud structure that once kept guard
overlooks the nearby tower with its silent bells
while Gunwharf and the Hard
hustle and bustle with a constant droning roar.

Broad shoulders hunched against the acid bite,
the mighty gate is serving as a door.

Like a limestone moon with its orbit settled,
its face cannot be seen. In days of horse and cobble
it was a guiding star, now tarred and metalled
roads cover the tracks that led away
to the villages that dotted this little island.

Farms and windmills, wheat and hay,
now streets and houses, shops and shopping mall.

The gate is still magnificent,
enjoying its periodic dose of oval and cricket ball;
retired, neglected, watching the sun on its climb
over the sprawl and haze of countless days,
a symbol of optimism as rousing as the Pompey Chime.

It follows the daily arc across the sky without regret,
through centuries of change, year upon year,
dawn upon dawn, rise upon rise, never having to see it set.

The Landport Gate was the principal entrance into the fortified town of Portsmouth and is the only town gate still in its original position.

The Pompey Chimes were recently restored and the bells are no longer silent

Dog Roses
(Jewish Cemetery, Fawcett Road, Southsea)

Cutting through side streets
I found, by chance

the small Jewish cemetery,
row on row of grey headstones;

the dead lowered down gently
on land leased for a thousand years.

Remembering how racists had
daubed paint, desecrated graves,

I stand staring through locked gates
in strong sunlight.

Bitterness still blew here
on this hot June afternoon,

the band of scarlet dog roses
caught in the coil of barbed wire

which crowned the wall,
daring anyone to spurn their flesh.

Portsmouth Cathedral

Here is the redundant font
the only
perpendicular piece
in the church,
now used
as a water
stoop

and here
are the war dead;
a book of names;
Handle, Holder,
Hoare
and white gloves
with which to
turn the page.

Here is the nave,
the place
where long ago
I would
hit the high notes,
raise the roof
in song.

Poised between birth
and death
I stop –
listening for
the girl
who once
made the rafters
ring.

St Stephen's Chapel
(North End, Buckland)

It was nearly five years after D-Day,
the twelfth of February 1949;
they gathered at the small chapel
in sight of the bombed-out ruin
of St Stephen's Church.

Nobody had a camera,
the image of my newly-wed parents
was never captured.

The high arched doorway
with its floral terracotta tiling
framed the happy couple
as they took their first steps
into the brave new world.

In time, the chapel was abandoned,
lost, and built over
by a 1950s department store
where it slept in the darkness
behind plasterboard panels
and bricked up doors.

Until 2004,
when for a brief month
it was revealed
when the shopfront was torn away
for redevelopment.

As the glass and plastic crumbled,
the plaster and brick bulldozed
into clouds of dust,
St Stephen's Chapel emerged.

With my camera I framed the image:
the high proud roof,
the frieze of brickwork that bands the wall
and the archway
and the tiles
still bright and neat above the door.

St Stephen's Chapel
survived the blitz to span three centuries,
clung to life for a few short weeks
as its fate was decreed:
to follow the bomb ravaged
mother church, its body savaged
by machines.

I walked away
with a heart as heavy
as the dusty terracotta flower
that I cradled in my hands.

Japanese Garden

Southsea's Rose Garden
honours our Cockleshell
heroes in colour and scent.
But lift

your flower-drugged face, look
through the hedge, see the
rarely-raked gravel and lonely
boulders

of the Japanese Garden, opened
by Maizuru's Mayor years ago
in honour of East-West
friendship.

Then, Mount Fuji proudly erupted,
topped with snowy splashes,
enriched by incontinent
seagulls.

Now, a wooden bridge
spans bald, dry pebbles,
its symbolism
forgotten.

The Spinnaker Tower

The Spinnaker Tower, the Spinnaker Tower,
we watched it grow taller, hour by hour.
The top of its structure began its ascent,
rising each day as they poured the cement.
The legs came together, uniting as one,
at three sixty-feet, the pouring was done.

Then came the trunnion to join the steel bows
supporting the platforms in parallel rows.
At three-thirty feet there is a glass floor
to see down below what's on the shore.
Up fifteen feet, the deck is enclosed
to keep out the wind, and not feel exposed.
The topmost of decks gives a view that is clear,
it's open to wind which whips past your ear.

Completing the top is a long slender spire,
increasing the height one-fifty feet higher.

Now that it's open, the visitors flock
and pay entrance fees, to get it out of hock.
They tell all their friends of the marvellous views,
and they in turn come: it's wonderful news.

JACQUELINE GABBITAS

Lubber

If the wind in my face was always salty, the ground beneath me half-given
to sand or shale, 'spinnaker' would always be the first *sp* word that comes to
mind. I'm making excuses. I'm not cut out for the sea. Wait, I can tie knots,
though! Clove hitch, sheep shank – I can't get the hang of reef knots but maybe
there's time. Hope yet. I can run a line to a rusting metal pole. Crossing,
slipping, passing the twine through the intersect. It's secure and good. You can
measure against it to get, just right, the height of a new-built wall (new-built
from old stones). The twine is blue. That blue, the one that surrounded us the
day in the Spinnaker Tower when we almost pretended to be local but didn't
in the end and paid. The blue that greeted us with its thumbs up when we
took a lift, and then walked some, then went through the out-door coming in
(it didn't mind we entered through an egress!) It was good, accommodating,
friendly, come-back-again blue. And it supported us, as we walked over the
glass floor and didn't feel like we were walking on air because the glass was
cold and slippery under our socks. Come on, it said, that blue, come on. There
you go. That was good wasn't it? You did well.

The Song of the Queen's Hotel

I am the Queen's Hotel
Like a beached liner
Right-angled to the sea,
> Quirkily

I am honey-coloured,
Six storeys tall,
And stories I could tell
> Curmudgeonly

I came with Victorians.
Now my attics are unused
Except by mice and spiders.
Once my servants lived up there
Next to my gabled roof
And now the Sunday lunches
Cost a footman's wages
> Extortionately

Now I have rooms for conferences
And business men, and my waiters
Come from across the sea
And chambermaids
Attend to my needs and penetrate
My crevices
> Reluctantly

Few lovers have trysts in my rooms
No infants toddle down my corridors
Still my windows look out to sea
And at the stately floating hotels
> Self-pityingly

Another Queen's reign draws to an end
No smart carriages disgorge at my door,
No fashionable ladies in bustles and big hats
Throng to take tea
> Chattily

My plaster pinnacles are cracking,
Soiled by gulls and dwarfed by the Tower
I hear the roar of four-by-fours
And I'm still here
> Surprisingly.

The Guildhall Clock

The Guildhall Clock chimed 12 o'clock; it also chimed at three
It chimed again at 5 o'clock when it was time for tea.

But then it stopped in wartime when bombs blew up the lot
The 'Play Up Pompey' melody was very soon forgot.

But hark, good news has come our way; it was in the evening News:
A new bell's going to be installed; it's been a long time due.

And so good Portsmouth people; let all of us rejoice
The heart of our great city has been given back its voice.

The Pompey Chimes: silenced by the bombs which gutted the Guildhall in 1941; rung by hand after the war to announce the peace; Guildhall restored 1959, but the bells broke down in 2003; restored again in 2009.

My Favourite Place

My favourite place in Southsea
is within a small brick wall.
There are lots of flowers and all sorts of colours.
At the moment they are
purple, white and cherry red in one bed
then they are yellow and sunset red
in the next.
There are benches everywhere,
a neat path for smooth with-wheels toys.
Trees of all sorts, big bushy ones;
small palm-tree-like ones.
The grass is thick green,
sprinkles of daisies all over.
The buildings are all smart and polished.
Sound is so quiet if you hear anything
it would be the soft
buzzing of a bee.
Smells so new so fresh so sweet,
for all the colours are there.
Feels so comfy on the grass
I could sleep.

(Talia Glanville, then aged 8)

Southsea Postcards

I.
In Wimbledon Road's little park,
where I know the dogs by name
and their owners by their dogs,
Lulu's owner said that her granddaughter's dad
forgot his Parental Contact Order that weekend.
She was glad to have the girl a bit longer
and there were tears behind her glasses.

II.
In the Albert Road fruit and veg shop
where the big woman is thumping tomatoes
onto the scales as if they were potatoes,
an old-young man in sandals complains about sell-by dates.
He takes a blackened banana and wolfs it.
'Against the law, this stuff, too old,' he says.
He takes another, adds: 'Older is sweeter. Like you.'

III.
Outside Waitrose early this winter morning
while the gutters cough and splutter the night's storm,
five shoppers in sleek coats chat till the doors open.
Just inches from the backs of ten shiny heels,
a mother rat cajoles her shivering infant, to dive
out of sight, quick, through the metal grating
into the swirling drain. Swim, baby rat, for your life.

The Surprise

Bricks. The simplicity of their form,
their basic oblong shape, their weight,
the heavy dependability.
This was a constant fascination to the boy.

Primary-coloured hard wooden blocks
were his first introduction; a means to create a solid wall,
maybe add a simple square doorway
with a leaden sentry on guard.

The plastic interlocking shapes followed:
the houses with windows and chimneys,
back gates, garden paths of mosaic leading to roads
of grey ribbon and black slate.

1960: the low back wall of the council estate
became his writing desk, his draughtsman's easel;
the mortar pointing held his pencils and pens
as he took in the complexity of his task.

So, how could he capture with crayon and ink
the absolute wonder of these bricks?
They were alive, they were a deep bottle green
full of intricate runs and links, they shone.

They gathered sunlight and released it
with a slow teasing glow. This was a palace,
a Taj Mahal, a green glazed vision and he
was entrusted with the mission of absorbing it.

Peel away the image in his eyes like a paper transfer,
slide it wet and newborn to the waiting folds
of an empty page. This was his challenge,
the bricks were waiting; he took strength from their wisdom.

The Surprise Pub in Landport, now demolished

Terraced Houses in Stamshaw, circa 1960

In summer's twilight over Stamshaw the soft light
illuminates the wise bearded slow moving clouds
ragging into ribbons above roof slate and firewall,
gutters that sag, cracked stone paving,
windows that glint over lace.
The pitted road ripples with shadowy people.

SUE LEGOOD

North End

I moved to Portsmouth in 65,
North End was oh! so very much alive.
Through Laburnum Grove, for me a short hop,
Then, all day, bliss! I could shop, shop, shop!

McIlroys — three floors of dresses to wear.
Melanies crammed with household wares.
Weston Hart the electrical store.
Messengers, for the rings I adore.

Boots the Chemist sold pills for your ills,
Dewhurst, with meat your basket could fill.
Freeman Hardy Willis sold shoes galore.
Young and Whites had beds for your snore!

Smith and Vosper sold cakes for your tea.
Victor Value fed the family.
Marks and Sparks sold bras by the score.
Woolworths then was packed to the door.

Southdown office if you wanted a trip.
The Thatched House if you felt like a nip.
The library, shelves full of books to read.
Chocolate King was a treat indeed.

Gaumont and Odeon for a film show.
Buses at the Corporation Depot.
Bulpitts soon had its final sale,
Vollers too told a similar tale.

Estate agents who once did so well
Now have only empty stores to sell.
QS and Peacocks both reign supreme,
But charity shops are the new regime.

Locksway Road

They called it Lily Lane
Every summer it was
thick with convolvulus,
a network of twining stems
hard to eradicate.

People pale as flowers
passed this way.
To contain the 'white scourge'
the council staked out
a sanatorium.

From their windows
patients felt the fresh, salt air
sweetening their lungs.
Watched the scroll of sea
unfurling their fate.
Saw the ivory moon,
the russet sun.

The red brick building still stands,
a family home now.
A sea breeze billows
white, lace curtains.
Only a hint of hospital remains.
A few iron palings
and the lilies in the lane.

Locksway Road, first called 'Asylum Road' after the TB sanatorium, later became known as 'Lily Lane'.

Underworld

South Parade Pier mid-November
peeling paintwork, empty promenade
flecks of silver in scales of rain
wind moaning around a rusting ribcage
the low lament of the distant drowned
in shifting shells of ships at sea

Through rotting hulks beneath the Solent
the dead rise up from cold mud beds
and swim with bass just under the surface
with opal skin and diamond eyes
they force white fingers through cresting waves
to stroke the sides of hulls that pass

In Gilman Lane

Glow worms
burn so brightly
competing with street lamps.
Who would expect to find them here in
Portsmouth?

Backwaters

we are walking

over thin sheets of time

The Small Fields
(Hilsea Creek)

Agrimony in the small fields —
the footpath tracks the ditch
bordering the creek;

delicate yellow spears
among fat swishes of blue sea-grasses,
each blade the owner of rich sea-shanties,

each individual stem has a name,
tiny clusters of small florets
breathe open.

Pollen swathes wrap round your face
this place breathes,
you want to go home, but the spears

beguile you, the grasses chant songs.
You are intoxicated by the sway of wind
throughout these small fields.

I think it might be the sun on yellow petals
that blinds your eyes to the footpath;
was there a footpath along this edge?

Somehow the thrum of the nearby creek
echoes in the soles of your feet.
You cannot leave now;

you are tightly-tethered as the gypsies' horses
nibbling sweet grasses.

A Little Reserve in Copnor

Folks often say 'it's grim up north', at the turning of the year.
When winter winds sweep Pompey, it's pretty grim down here.
Reluctantly, I set out for the obligatory walk,
none of us dog walkers is going to stop and talk.
I'm sure the dogs would rather stay curled up by the fire
than trail round the reserve, in the ice and the mire.
The foxes and rabbits stay deep underground,
and the seagulls' sad cry is a most desolate sound.

Then suddenly it's spring; the grey skies clear,
young families and old folk all come flocking here.
Footballs, bikes, scooters and kites come out for an airing,
rabbits scamper, dogs frolic, all nature is sharing
the warmth and the blossom, the trees in young green,
the birds' courting rituals as they flutter and preen.

Then somnolent summer all drowsy with heat,
ambling and gossiping with friends that we meet.
There's a skylark trilling way up high,
just a tiny black dot in a bright blue sky.
Rescued horses come to the fence as I come into view.
They know I always carry an apple or two.
Two resident sheep, Hope and Petal by name,
prance down the field to join in this game.
They don't want apples or carrots, despise cabbages too:
But Weetabix, digestive biscuits and rich tea will do.

We hope for an Indian summer when autumn rolls around
Acorns, conkers, sycamore keys join the leaves on the ground.
There used to be wild plum trees, nobody knew they were there
Admiral Lord Nelson School got built – the branches now are bare.
I wish I knew more about fungi, all shapes and sizes about,
But can't tell a cep from a deathcap, so they're safe for another year.

Everyone knows of the *Victory* and the *Mary Rose* close at hand
follies built out in the sea, towers and castles on land
to be marveled at, and our naval heritage second to none.
There's Gunwharf and the Dockyard, look over them one by one.
When you've seen all of these and would like to relax
It's way north to Copnor you must make your tracks:
there you'll find a secret wild life nature reserve
where you can stroll freely, or just sit and observe.

haiku

at the back of the old theatre
a pair of foxes
in the rubble

Chris Sparkes

how startlingly white
the gulls are, butting into
this devilish wind!

Eric Speight

screeching laughing gulls
circle round the old harbour
– spirits of the town

Chris Sparkes

wintry sun
and over the deserted funfair
a gull, soaring

Michael Gunton

February fog
the voices of gulls come from
over the water

Martin Lucas

stationed on the outpost
of a litter-bin, a seagull
letting out his throat-corroded yells

Chris Sparkes

swimming inland, the
milky tide brings seaweed. Three
black shags on a dead ash

Hugh Dunkerley

dawn sun
half-hidden by low cloud;
a ragged heron

Martin Lucas

the train shakes, blasts the
moment. The swans lift, kicking
loose of the water

Hugh Dunkerley

just above the cars
heavy swans
struggle for height

Denise Bennett

Journey with the Dog

We take the pathway alongside the moat,
moorhens, water-rail and coots glide
in leaf-brown water.

Follow as it narrows towards a pond –
a bomb crater, from sixty years ago,
now swans and egrets peck sedges.

Crunch under the railway bridge,
feet wet, trains – slips of light
cruise over us and out over the creek.

A muddy footpath, and we are walking
over thin sheets of time covering an airfield,
where Tiger-moths and Dakotas once purred;

my father worked here building war planes.
Now a housing estate lays a transfer
over ruler-straight runways.

Turn onto a cycle-route,
cross the roundabout into Marconi – a factory
where thousands of people work out of sight.

Over Norway Road rail bridge, through a busy
industrial estate, find squeezed into one corner
a footpath tracking alongside Victorian Ramparts.

One hour of walking –
kingfishers stoke winter trees.
We are nearly home.

The Foxes

That scream
at first we thought a baby's cry!

I imagined them
in a velvet sheen of darkness
down some desperate side alley
back of the bins off London Road
between the scraps and cyanide caps
seizing their morsel of pleasure.

And afterwards they'd pick the bones
together from some rancid carcass
and slope away along the conduit
alert for rats.

Tough love
when every dream is toxic
and every thought expects betrayal.

Pompey Fox

All those helpers.
He don't give a toss.
He just wants to get
the flea out his ear
the worm out his butt.
Nine, ten, eleven
magpies and crows
nosey interrupting.

He yawns and walks off
stiff with a low tail.
They gather around
once more looking
hopping, consulting
blameless, full of eyes.

Starlings at Eastney

On the shore
sailing boats moored up for winter
are strung with black bunting:
birds on the rigging
in dark, glossy suits,
a pit full of musicians
tuning up for an overture —
below, scooting by the surf
a tea party of starlings plays
catch me if you can,
beaks full of bread
and cake crumbs.

In the distance the Hayling Ferry
comes crabbing through
rough water.

The Kingfisher

Not looking far enough ahead –
too concerned with keeping on my feet,
from stumbling on the rubbled
towpath and falling into the creek,
I almost missed the kingfisher:
just saw a tiny speck of light
leaving the safety of the hawthorn;
short, snappy notes alerting my eyes.

Now I'm looking out over the water
towards the motorway
and just where evening traffic
stagnates, blue diamond wings
rapidly beat the air,
tracing an erratic flight-path,
slipping under the railway bridge
towards the estuary.

Cuckoo
(often heard in Tangier Road)

Today he sings at four in the morning
on the waste ground on the edge of the city,
calling his hussif hen.
Later, she will drop her eggs wide,
leave others to rear her young.

How many summers ago
did my children play here —
they and four others, all boys,
caught in the mesh of long grass,
sun splashing through the trees,
the salt wind whipping their kites.
Days when the go-cart went like a Ferrari,
pram wheeling, spinning out of control
and the reek and sting of hot nettles
brought squinnies for a dock leaf;
days when we scanned the sky for larks,
the ground for fox tracks and once,
when we found the full fury of a wasps's nest.
And always the drama of Sherwood Forest
when the only girl commanded her merry men
making her brother play a maid.

How many times did I herd them home:
Little John, Will Scarlet, Friar Tuck
the Sheriff of Nottingham, to cool in the splash pool
swapping bags of gold for lemonade and cake.
Their friends are now big-billy-goats-gruff —
but they still speak, still knock my door
for me to sign a passport photo —
write a testimonial.

Today he sings again behind the terraced houses,
he and his hussif hen courting.

GLEN JAYSON

Whispers
(Southsea Rose Garden)

Whispers and echoes float around the roses.
Fragrances titillate the senses.
Harboured by old walls, we're strengthened by the past
And a plaque remembers
Cockleshell Heroes

Regulars sit, come rain or shine
Starting their day with inspiration.
The atmosphere is tranquil with silent prayers
Thanking the sun, the clouds, the rain.
Thanking life.

Blind woman, arthritic man and tourists have their favourites
But here is my rose, blazing peach indefinable.
The gardener says these petals are the last to feel the frost
And so many people like to sit close.
I ask its name, then nod a smile:
The most popular rose is called
'Whispers'.

An Hour Moved On

Creek walk, an hour later than usual,
there is an emptiness
of humans, animals and birds,
as though this segment of time
belongs to hedges and trees,
while they try to resemble creatures,
try to converse with each other.

Then, one man walking
is enough for me to change direction.
His ankles may be dragging tree roots,
his hands, barbed thorns,
eyes spangled with luminous berries —
see inside my head,
while he is caught in this barbarous state.

He resembles a shackled man on death-row
walking into another dimension,
no last minute reprieve,
unlike Hezekiah's awesome reward
of fifteen extra years,
when God sealed his pledge;

set the shadow on the sun dial
at dusk, back ten steps.
We would tear the earth apart
trying to explain such phenomena;
the shackled man re-use each minute
as God intended.

My City

you can be somebody in Portsmouth...

Anchor-shaped Island

You great salty vessel, you anchor-shaped island,
You marsh-harboured flat in the sight of the Hill,
The morning is rouging your Wighted horizon,
Your roundabouts hiss and your waders are still.
Remembered memorials freshen their guano
While overners shram in the hovercraft bay,
And deep in the yolk of a Korner Kaff breakfast
Commercial Road precinct embraces the day.

I sailed in the bus past the bingo at Cosham,
The peeling facades of the clubs at North End,
I dreamed, mid the nicotine laundries of Stamshaw,
The Fratton retreats and the Hard round the bend,
And out through the Camber, the ferry, the funfair,
Where *Mary Rose* sank and the *Victory* was mine,
I dreamed of dry-docking, of dropping my moorings,
But waves bore me out to a world left behind.

Oh cider-skinned innocence, pleasure-pier teen years,
Stuck out in the Solent, encrusted and cool,
My pub and my factory, my night-shifty vac job,
My public, detested, suspended-from school,
Oh southernmost gateway of windy dominion,
And great shifting world, you're entirely my own,
My past shaping present, my wanderer's birthplace,
My cradle, my sailor, my Portsmouth, my home.

NAOMI WODDIS

Everywhere the Taste of Salt

*(poetry mosaic made from epigrams posted at Gunwharf Quays for
'Voyage East', Chinese New Year celebrations, 2009)*

I made a wish to fly and landed here.
A wall of glass opened a whisper's width,
just enough for me to pass through
and make this place my home.

All the front doors are painted
the same colour. Our house
is a Bangladeshi house. Inside
is where we make our signature.

Portsmouth gives me sunshine,
the scattering of stars on water,
days and night bleed
into one another. Everywhere

the taste of salt. Their words are hard
to understand. It can be lonely
to talk with just your hands,
the look on your face.

Eat this, she says, it tastes of the sea.
Unwrapping the paper I find
the golden heart of cod in batter,
sink my teeth into a brand new day.

Abroad

It didn't matter that everything was grey.
Smoke and slate grey touching a sea green
and brown grey, foamed at the water's
surface with dead souls' icy spray. Mama
had packed me an extra jumper, rye bread
with poledwica. And in the fog I saw
the ship – swashbuckle silver – counted
her guns, wet metal grey. Days after that
I'd play captain, pacing her quarter deck
with my musket; I'd light stern lanterns
on her poop deck, shout orders to the wind
as we steered through choppy water.

Instead of sailing her we went across
on the ferry. It didn't matter. It was enough
to hear gulls shriek, feel the brine's
taunting slap, see foam crash
in our wake. We leaned overboard as far
as we dared till the teacher yanked
us back by our anoraks.

I've been to the port, I shouted
we saw the tall ships, we sailed abroad!
There were no words for the seal grey,
cross-bone and skull white
marbled grey, only a smell of diesel
in my hair, the sting of the spray
still cold on my cheeks. Mama took
my wet clothes. This isn't home,
we're already abroad was all she said.

My Portsmouth

I, your new folk
        blackened by the African sun
        a stowaway
        from yonder African ports
        I salute you
        great admiral of Northern seas

Portsmouth
        of histories ancient and modern
        of queens stern, regal and victorious
        of wars fought and won
        purveyor of sons brave and strong
        daring the sea gales
        riding hurricanes
        for glory, for honour, for justice
        great port of the South
        I salute you

Portsmouth
        a barrel of humanity
        curries, roasts, noodles, chips, taramosalatas
        nibbles from afar and nigh
        ales, wines, waragis, vodkas, rums
        tipples from any shore
        delight palates
        drifting into your opulent store
        I salute your Southern breast
        great port of Britain

Portsmouth, my Portsmouth,
        of churches aplenty
        of pubs never far away
        of markets bursting with wares
        Zambian roses, Italian clothes, Egyptian potatoes
        Swiss watches, Argentinian apples, British what?

Portsmouth
        of private gardens, rose gardens, public gardens
        your theatres re-live human histories
        while Portsmouth Football Club
        kicks up a heady ball
        for the world to cry
        Long Live Pompey!
                     Kampala, Uganda

ROWLAND LEE
(1945 – 2010)

A Farewell to Dave

In order to stop cruelty to animals
Dave Perry (a vegetarian) has volunteered himself
for the meat raffle at the Red, White and Blue next Friday.
First prize is Dave's leg.
Second prize is Dave's bum – a nice piece of rump steak.
All the rest of him is going into sausages.

So – a short poem:
> Farewell to Dave
> A Brave Man

See you Dave – I won't be eating you myself –
I don't like sausages.

From Ryde Pier Head

Across the impossible blue
of an August sea
Portsmouth glints and gleams
glitters golden in the haze.

Seems to me
there can't be many days
when Portsmouth,
fighting drunk on summer sun

can get away
with fooling anyone
that it's some sort of enchanted kingdom —
        but this is one of them.

Salt Islands

Winter was the landscape of my island,
bitter winds, late afternoons, the wet brash
of salt and rain flaying me, making my skin sing.
I was afloat in my father's isolation
held on the surf side of this other island,
pinned furthest from the road that led away
and now leads back again.

I was not the only one to notice
the process of the storm's diffusion
as water and the skyline became one,
odd days, storms cutting clean across horizons
until the calm (as it always did)
stitched it together. Fine scars.
Continual separation, suspension, division.

There were balmier days, hotter summers
than these now are, earlier mornings wading
as the tide was turning in my favour.
It was safe then. And later evening
immersions, buoyed by the same salt
only sighing, while tiny silver fish
flashed around me, luminescent, strange, silent.

Now the sound of the sea when I hear it
comes as if my head is laid on his chest
as it was in the beginning and at the end.
Salt still drives the back of my throat.
The island lies in Winter, permanent,
while inland, gulls remind me that water
is never far away on an island.

Flood Zone

English floodwaters are grey and slow:
the road sign and car door measure depth.
We bought a house in the flood zone: surely no risk
of a wall of water up the Channel and into the Solent
from some deep Atlantic mountain drop?

Here the sea will slowly ooze
along the brown muddy Common,
fill the vacant basement flats,
inch up the railings in Wimbledon Park.
From our first floor window, we'll smell
the ever closer line of seaweed and shells,
and hear the pebbles rake the tree trunks.
We're just a smaller island now, we'll say.

Waterside City
(a group poem)

The smell of fuel from the boats in the harbour
The smell of adventure
From the fish market, the smell of rotten fish
And garbage, the smell of dew on grass
The smell of flowers and holly leaves:
The sea wind takes all the smells away
Up into the thick salty air, the soft clouds.
It smells like home to me.

The Spinnaker Tower is a tall tree that touches the sky.
Walking on The Square Hole makes my heart beat faster,
It's like walking on thin air: Petrifying!
But it's also like flying - like a dream.
See the island swim like a colourful fish
See a rainy day turn bright.
It looks like home to me.

Smell the cafe drinks and coffee beans,
Smell the delicious sea air. Taste a lolly,
a chock chip ice cream: taste the pink
candyfloss from the funfair.
It tastes like home to me.

Walking on the bumpy beach, playing on the stones,
Is like walking on salty, crunchy crisps. Water trickles
Through my toes and tickles the pebbles. Cars zoom by
Like a herd of crabs doing the tango. Waves splash,
Or twirl and crash on a rainy day. Seagulls clack.
It sounds like home to me.

I hear rain on my classroom window,
See a rainbow fading above the school field.
I feel safe when I think about Portsmouth.
It feels like home to me.

My Town

I feel
that you can be
somebody in Portsmouth.
You can stride around it —
almost own it.

I feel
that you can be
somebody in Portsmouth.
The folk who walk around it seem
to own it.

Bennett, Denise: 'The Salvation Army Lady', poem film, Chichester University, 2009; 'Journey', *Acumen;* 'Company of Flowers', Dog Roses' and Emma Hamilton speaks', *South Magazine*

Ford, Robin: 'Pompey Town', *South Magazine*

Gunthorp, Dale: 'Southsea Postcards', *Candelabrum Poetry Magazine,* Red Candle Press, London and Portsmouth, October 2009

Jacobs, Peter: 'The History of Me', Elaine Crinnion's Wordclub, 2005-7

Harvey, W.J.: 'Portsmouth', *Poems of the Second World War: The Oasis Selection,* Everyman Library, J.M. Dent, London, 1958.

Hessey, Ben: 'Noises', Elaine Crinnion's Wordclub, 2005

Hawkesworth, Pauline: 'An Hour Moved On', *Bracken Women in Lime Trees,* Indigo Dreams Press, Ross-on-Wye, 2009

Haynes, John: 'St James's Hospital', *Ashes,* Arvon Anthology, 2000 and *Daily Telegraph*

Henry, Michael: 'Pompey Chimes' and 'The Night Fishermen' in *After the Dancing Dogs,* Enitharmon Press, London, 2008; 'Pompey Chimes' also in *Celebration: An anthology...Cheltenham Poetry Society,* Trimingham Press, 1998 and *Tears in the Fence,* No. 39, Autumn 2004, Blandford Forum; 'On Southsea Esplanade' in *Time Haiku* (Issue 10,) 1999, London

Hill, David: 'Anchor-shaped Island', *Literary Review,* London, September 2001, 'Cup of Tea', *Art Force,* Liverpool, September 2001; 'The Animals', Poem Film, Chichester University, 2009

Hull, Robert: 'On Portsmouth Station' in *On Portsmouth Station,* Beafred, Salisbury, 2008; poem film, Chichester University, 2009

Jones, Ken: 'All's right on the night', commemorating the Tongues & Grooves poetry and music concert at the New Theatre Royal, 2006

McCarthy, M. L.: 'Exiled in the City', *Pleasure is Lonely,* Spinnaker Press, Portsmouth, 2010, and *Candelabrum Poetry Magazine,* Red Candle Press, Portsmouth, April 2010;

Marsh George: haiku, poem films, Chichester University, 2009

Marsh, George: Kensit, Connaire; Mills, Sally; Goulden, Milly, Sparkes, Chris; Speight, Eric; Gunton, Michael; Lucas, Martin; Dunkerley, Hugh; Bennett, Denise, Rollinson, Anthony; Ficton, Mia; Bell, David: the haiku from these poets were previously published in *Into the small hours ... Portsmouth in haiku,* British Haiku Society, Portsmouth Branch, 1994

Mathewson, Anna: 'Lover', *Noir et Blanc* magazine

Missellbrook, Ron: 'That Summer Afternoon' Poem Film, Chichester University, 2009; Angel Radio FM.

Nelson, Katie: 'On Eastney Beach', Elaine Crinnion's Wordclub, 2007

Norgate, Stephanie: 'Night ferries', poem film, Chichester University, 2009

Olesker, Stuart: 'I'm Tom Ellis Owen', from The *'Ouses in Between,* a music hall entertainment about the life of Owen by Stuart Olesker and John Stanton

Perryment, Michael: 'The Ragbone Man', winner, Tongues&Grooves Poetry Competition, 2006. 'The Lady of the Lake', commended in the same competition

Ross, Alan: 'Slow Train to Portsmouth', *Alan Ross Poems,* ed. David Hughes, Harvill Press, London, 2005

Rudd, Andrew: 'A View of the Ferries', *One Cloud away from the Sky,* Cheshire County Council, 2007; Second prize, Ledbury Poetry Competition, 2004

Sawkins, Maggie: 'A Sort of Bargaining', winner Ottaker's Poetry Competition, 2003; 'Cold Harbour', version in *Brittle Star,* Issue Twenty One; 'Teaching English at Friendship House', published as 'Elimination' in *The Zig Zag Woman,* Two Ravens Press 2007.

Scriven, John: 'Resurrection Day on Milton Common', Poem Film, Chichester University, 2009

Simpson, Mercer: 'Naval Engagement', *Early Departures, Late Arrivals,* Rockingham Press, Ware, Herts; 'A Sheltered Upbringing', part II, *Rain from a Clear Blue Sky,* Gomer Press, Dyfed, Wales, 1994;

Sparkes, Chris: 'Founder's Day', *Be Still and Know,* Blue Butterfly, Aberdeenshire, 2007

Stocks, Jon: 'The Foxes', *Candelabrum Poetry Magazine,* April 2009, London and Portsmouth

Torrington, Tricia: 'Untitled Pharmacy', *The Opium Fish,* Flarestack, 2010; winner Stroud Open Poetry Competition 1992. 'Portsea', prizewinner Ottaker's Poetry Competition, 2002; poem film by Chichester University, 2009; it and 'Desiderata' in *The Opium Fish* and in The Road to Cherington, Kingscourt Press, 2008. 'Awareness of White' and 'Salt Islands' *Lodestones, 2001: The Border Poets,* Five Seasons Press, UK.

'Everywhere the taste of salt' by Naomi Woddis: thanks due to John Sackett, Portsmouth Chinese Association and Kam Ip

This book includes poems from disadvantaged groups, including excluded school children and the mental health community. Some were linked with Tongues&Grooves poetry workshops.